Elder Zenobius

Elder Zenobius

A Life in Spiritual Continuity with Pre-revolutionary Russia

Zenoviy Chesnokov
Translated from the Russian by Sophia Moshura

Holy Trinity Publications
The Printshop of St Job of Pochaev
Holy Trinity Monastery
Jordanville, New York
2013

Printed with the blessing of His Eminence,
Metropolitan Hilarion, First Hierarch
of the Russian Orthodox Church Outside of Russia

Elder Zenobius © 2013 Zenoviy Chesnokov

HOLY TRINITY PUBLICATIONS
The Printshop of St Job of Pochaev
Holy Trinity Monastery
Jordanville, New York 13361-0036
www.holytrinitypublications.com

ISBN: 978-0-88465-331-8 (paperback)
ISBN: 978-0-88465-350-9 (ePub)
ISBN: 978-0-8846-5351-6 (Kindle)

Library of Congress Control Number 2013938141

CONTENTS

INTRODUCTION

The life of Metropolitan Zenobius of Tetritzkaro was completely dedicated to serving the Holy Orthodox Church and his neighbors. There are people whose names remain long in the hearts and prayers of believers. Such a grace-filled person, who acquired the gifts of the Holy Spirit, was His Eminence Metropolitan Zenobius.

Patriarch Ilia II, Catholicos-Patriarch of All Georgia,
at Metropolitan Zenobius's burial service on March 14, 1985[1]

On August 21, 2010, at the Divine Liturgy in the Glinsk Hermitage of the Nativity of the Mother of God (located in the village of Sosnovka, Glukhovski district, Sumskaya region) three great ascetics of the twentieth century were canonized: Schema-Metropolitan Seraphim (Metropolitan Zenobius Mazhuga), Schema-Archimandrite Seraphim (Romantzov), and Schema-Archimandrite Andronicus (Lukash), who carried their monastic obedience at the hermitage.

The Divine Liturgy was served by His Beatitude Metropolitan Vladimir of Kiev and All Ukraine. Many people who knew these great elders gathered at the monastery that day and came to honor their labors for Christ's Church. Many of those present at the canonization were their spiritual children who testify in their memoirs to the elders' powerful prayer and clairvoyance.

After the last panikhida, the reasons for canonization, as adopted by the Holy Synod of the Ukrainian Orthodox Church, were read aloud, as were the lives of the new saints. Then, during the singing of the troparion, kontakion, and the megalynarion of the newly canonized saints, their icons were carried out of the altar to be venerated. At the end of the service, Metropolitan Vladimir congratulated the faithful on the glorification of the Glinsk ascetics and wished them the elders' prayerful intercession before God.

At the conclusion of the service, Metropolitan Andrey of Samtaviysk and Goriysk (Georgia) appealed to the multitude of faithful by stressing the importance of the Glinsk elders' deeds and works for the spiritual unity of Orthodox Christians around the world (the elders served for many years in Georgia). "These ascetics were the spiritual fathers of many Ukrainians, Russians, Georgians, Greeks, and Armenians who came to them," said the Georgian hierarch. "And today their intercession has become even broader and more fertile—they pray for us all. Therefore, on this day the Georgian Church rejoices together with the Ukrainian Church and all of God's people."

The Glinsk Hermitage, where exercise in prayer was traditionally united with preaching and material help to all who came, produced an entire constellation of elders, thirteen of whom were canonized in 2008. Most of these were ascetics who labored in the hermitage and whose sanctity was revealed by the famous miracles they had worked in the eighteenth and nineteenth centuries. Schema-Metropolitan Seraphim, Schema-Archimandrite Seraphim, and Schema-Archimandrite Andronicus survived until the closing of the Glinsk Hermitage in 1922. They had their share of persecution, exile, and imprisonment. Their advice and support was sought by the faithful from all over the former Soviet Union.

The decision to canonize the ascetics was made at a meeting of the Holy Synod of the Ukrainian Orthodox Church on March 25, 2009. The memory of the newly glorified saints began to be celebrated on the Synaxis of the Holy Glinsk Fathers on September 9/22.

This book is specifically concerned with the life and pastoral service of Metropolitan Zenobius (Mazhuga), in schema Seraphim.[2] The celebration of the twenty-fifth anniversary of Metropolitan Zenobius's repose on March 8, 2010, was marked in the Russian Orthodox Church's calendar that year in a list of notable dates. The anniversary was celebrated with great solemnity in the Glinsk Hermitage and in Georgia, where Elder Zenobius spent much of his life. A solemn liturgy was served in the St Alexander Nevsky Church in Tbilisi, where he served for thirty-five years. A good number of clergy and laity, many of whom were His Grace's spiritual children, gathered in the church. On the same day, his last cell attendant, now Archpriest Alexander Chesnokov, arrived from Krasnodar. After the Divine Liturgy a memorial service was led by His Holiness and Beatitude Catholicos-Patriarch Ilia, a spiritual son tonsured by Metropolitan Zenobius. The day before (March 7), the holy Catholicos-Patriarch noted that Metropolitan Zenobius spent most of his life in the Iberian land. "In the future, we will also have a canonization," he said.[3]

Vladyka Zenobius's bright path in life is best understood if considered together with the providential care of the Creator and the great gifts He gives to one who dedicates his entire life to serve Him. Saints have no national boundaries. While serving God and his neighbor throughout this earthly life, St Zenobius attained the "crown of righteousness," which gives us confidence that he has boldness before the throne of God, praying for his spiritual children and all those who call to him in prayer. During his life, Vladyka helped the monasteries existing on Georgian territory as much as possible, as well as a few convents in Russia and abroad. It is difficult to count the number of people who have found the path to spiritual salvation through Vladyka's paternal care. They always remember their spiritual father with gratitude.

People came from all corners of the earth to receive Vladyka's spiritual guidance. Many of those whom Vladyka Zenobius tonsured and ordained to this day carry pastoral obediences in various parishes of the Georgian Patriarchate and in the Russian Orthodox Church. Vladyka Zenobius brought up many worthy pastors. He continued the tradition of spiritual guidance, which began with St Paisius (Velichkovskiy) and continued with St Philaret (Danilevskiy) and other Glinsk elders. The Metropolitan and Elder Zenobius became a living link between eldership before the Russian revolution and eldership in the twentieth century. After the Glinsk Hermitage's closing, many of its elders were warmly welcomed by Vladyka Zenobius.

Metropolitan Zenobius kept in touch with the Trinity-Sergius Lavra and was close friends with Father Kirill (Pavlov).[4] If Vladyka

visited Moscow, he considered it his duty to visit the lavra and see
Father Kirill, who would return the favor whenever he would come
to the Caucasus. These meetings were photographed a few times,
including one included in this book. Vladyka was also well acquainted
with Father John (Krestiankin),[5] Father Seraphim (Tyapochkin),
and many other great elders. The elders connected with them not
only spiritually in prayer, but also whenever they met in person.

It is difficult to assess the importance of Vladyka Zenobius to
the Georgian Orthodox Church, for which he served and labored
for nearly half a century. This began in 1922, when he moved to the
Dranda Assumption Monastery in Abkhazia after the closing of the
Glinsk Hermitage. He lived through many of the most important historical events of our Church and State in the twentieth century. During
this period the Church survived persecution after the revolution, the
thaw following World War II, and the Khrushchev persecutions. With
God's help, Vladyka worthily overcame all of these trials. Vladyka
truly had the perfect combination of episcopal ministry and eldership.

During the writing of this book, much new information was
gathered and analyzed. Some ambiguities in the biography of the
saint—such as the exact dates of his stay in the Glinsk Hermitage
and the Caucasus Mountains, and the time of his arrest and places
of exile—were clarified in an autobiography and with various official government forms written by Vladyka himself, which were
found in the archives of the Georgian Patriarchate. Orders to give
ecclesiastical awards to Metropolitan Zenobius from the Moscow
and Georgian patriarchs were also found.

The author collected and recorded memories of St Zenobius's
spiritual children. Particularly valuable were the memories of His
Holiness and Beatitude Ilia II, since Vladyka spent most of his life
in Georgia. Thanks to the published and collected memoirs we
were able to shed light on various events in the elder-hierarch's life
and thus obtain a more detailed view of his pastoral ministry.

This book is divided into two parts. The first part relates the life
of St Zenobius, while the second describes his many-sided pastoral
ministry. The appendix contains reminiscences of church hierarchs,
clergy, and his spiritual children.

PART I

The Life of St Zenobius, Metropolitan of Tetritzkaro (in Schema Seraphim)

CHAPTER I

Childhood and Education

Metropolitan Zenobius (born Zachariah Ioakimovich[1] Mazhuga) was born on September 14/26, 1896,[2] in the town of Glukhov in the Chernigov Province (now the Sumskaya region) in a working class family. His father was a carpenter and his mother was a housewife. From early childhood, Zachariah had to endure many hardships. At age three his father died; at eleven, he lost his pious mother Theodosia, who brought him up in faith and love for God. He was always very attentive to all that surrounded him, so much so that his peers would jokingly call him a monk. According to eyewitnesses, when Vladyka Zenobius recalled his childhood, he mentioned that he did not see a reason for this nickname, even though he often went to the hermitage to carry out small tasks for the monks. He graduated from the parish school, yet because of his poverty he did not have the opportunity to study further.

After his parents' deaths, Zachariah lived in the home of his cousin Paraskeva. The family was large and poor, so it was hard to feed everyone. So when Zachariah was sixteen, Paraskeva gave the boy to the House of Work for peasant children at the Glinsk Hermitage. At this time, dozens of others of his own age with a similar background, the needy, and orphans studied various trades there. Boys were placed in workshops they chose themselves and for five years were taught their chosen craft: iconography, tailoring, shoemaking, carpentry, lathe operating, and others. This House of Work was established to give orphans an education and occupation so that they could make a living if they decided to live outside of the hermitage. The education was difficult. In addition to the chosen craft, boys were taught the Law of God, reading, church singing, and calligraphy. On Sundays and feast days the boys had to attend church services. With the boys in the House of Work lived a monk who watched their behavior and sought to educate them in the spirit of Orthodoxy. Upon entering the Glinsk Hermitage, Zachariah learned to sew. He was very glad to study there because he had repeatedly visited the hermitage and knew some of its inhabitants. He would run minor errands for the monks, who in turn would warm the orphaned boy's soul by showing him parental warmth and affection. Later, Vladyka Zenobius wrote that in the Glinsk Hermitage he "could freely grow spiritually, which left him grateful to the hermitage for the rest of his life." Processions from the Glinsk Hermitage to Glukhov and back with the miraculous icon of the Nativity of the Mother of God[3] left an indelible imprint on the soul of the God-fearing boy.

The Holy Theotokos gave Zachariah Her protection from childhood. The town of Glukhov had several churches and "twenty miles from the city were two monasteries: the Glukhov Peter and Paul Monastery for men and the Glukhov Assumption Monastery for women."[4] However, the Virgin Mary led Zachariah to the Glinsk Hermitage—an abode dedicated to Her Nativity. It so happened that all major events in the life of this great saint of God were tied with feasts of the Blessed Lady: "on the Nativity of the Holy Virgin he first saw the Glinsk Hermitage, on the day of the Annunciation he took monastic vows, and on the day of the Dormition of the Blessed Virgin [he] was released early from prison."[5]

CHAPTER 2

The Glinsk Hermitage:
In Obedience to the Elders

PATH TO THE GLINSK HERMITAGE

The Glinsk Hermitage, dedicated to the Nativity of the Mother of God, has long been famous for its elders no less than the Optina Hermitage. After the Optina Hermitage was destroyed in 1942, the Glinsk Hermitage carried the light of Christ's Truth to the world for nineteen years, as it was allowed to reopen between 1942 and 1961.

"The Glinsk Hermitage stood on the boundary of Russia and Ukraine, and was a part of the Kursk province, but due to the efforts of Nikita Khrushchev, this part of the Russian lands was ceded to the Sumsk province of Ukraine."[1] The hermitage was established in the sixteenth century by the grace of the Mother of God, through the miraculous icon of the Nativity of the Mother of God that appeared on a pine tree in the forest. Around this icon formed the Glinsk Hermitage, which by the end of the nineteenth century contained five churches, two sketes, four house-churches, fifteen buildings for the hermitage monks, eight guesthouses for pilgrims, a refectory, a laundry room, a hospital with a pharmacy, numerous household buildings that included four water mills, and the House of Work for orphan boys. There were more than four hundred monks dwelling in the hermitage. The hermitage was a powerful stronghold of Orthodoxy on Russia's southern border.

The miraculous icon of the Nativity of the Mother of God, whose appearance gave rise to the Glinsk Hermitage, is also called the "Pustynno-Glinskaya." The icon is not large, about six inches by eight inches. It shows the righteous Saints Joachim and Anna, and the little

5

Virgin Mary in Her mother's arms. These three images are separated
on the icon by specially designed borders. Over time, the icon was
decorated "in gold and adorned with precious stones. In addition,
there were silver 'decorations' that were presented in gratitude by
those who received healing. Such gifts on the miraculous icon were
always numerous."[2]

As the Glinsk Hermitage grew more prosperous, it became
more active in charitable work. At the end of the nineteenth century, the hermitage annually hosted up to 45,000 pilgrims. We also
know that by the beginning of the twentieth century this number
increased to 60,000. It is worth noting that in the late nineteenth to
early twentieth centuries the Glinsk Hermitage was in its prime. At
that time the hermitage was not only involved in charity, but it also
was involved in active missionary and educational work.

Throughout his life, young Zachariah's heart retained a love
for charity and mercy that he was taught at the hermitage. Loving Christ from his youth, he entered the Glinsk Hermitage of the
Nativity of the Mother of God in 1914 as a novice, making a firm
decision to follow the monastic path.

HIS SPIRITUAL FATHER: OBEDIENCE AND TRIALS

The novice Zachariah was put under the spiritual leadership of a
strict elder—Monk Gerasim. Their relationship was interesting and
providential. In the Glinsk Hermitage, everyone was under the spiritual patronage of an elder or a spiritually experienced monk. Having come to Father Gerasim, Zachariah knew that the elder chased
everyone away, and so he was ready for such a reception. The elder
ordered him to leave or else he would beat him with a stick. The
novice answered that even if he was beaten with a stick, he would not
go away until Father Gerasim agreed to become his spiritual mentor. Then the elder replied, "Now you are my spiritual son. I did so
with all and everyone left me, but you did not leave." From then on,
novice Zachariah followed his spiritual teachings and guidance, and
learned to be abstinent in words and food but generous in prayer.

Living under obedience to Elder Gerasim became the founda-
tion of Vladyka Zenobius's future spiritual formation. The young

novice had to endure many sorrows and difficulties, "but in order for adamant to turn into a diamond it needs careful polishing and painstaking work. Likewise the young novice, having passed through obedience in a coenobitic hermitage, learns that through patience and love for the brothers one wins over temptation."[3]

These words of Scripture were manifest in Zachariah: "My son, if you draw near to serve the Lord, prepare your soul for temptation. Set your heart right and be steadfast, and do not strive anxiously in distress. Cleave to Him and do not fall away, that you may be honored at the end of your life" (Sir 2:1–3). He was firmly convinced that he was on the true path, and the Lord, though He tested His faithful servant, did not leave him and helped him to grow in virtue.

The young man had different obediences: making prosphora, sewing in the tailor shop, and many others, but did not succeed anywhere, and so was transferred from place to place. Young Zachariah wanted to serve God, but he could not stay in one obedience for long. "He had cousins. His cousin, who lived in Kiev, often came with her husband to the hermitage and would try to persuade him to go and live with them."[4] Yet Zachariah, remembering that we must undergo many tribulations in order to enter God's kingdom (Acts 14:22), did not want to change his intentions and leave the hermitage.

The hermitage's abbot, Archimandrite Nectarios, foreseeing the young monk's great future, patiently moved him from one obedience to another. Everything normalized after Zachariah was given an obedience in the stables. He was afraid of horses and at first complained that he was removed from obediences where he could do at least something. Yet with God's help Zachariah began to carry out this obedience, eventually succeeding in it and beginning to lead a virtuous life.[5]

In 1914, World War I began. Russian monasteries assisted the Russian Empire both materially and in manpower. The Glinsk Hermitage also assisted the army and people during this difficult time. Father Nectarios sent hieromonks to serve as chaplains in the army, providing them with everything necessary for the soldiers' spiritual health. From 1915 to 1916, the Glinsk Hermitage sent seventy-five novices to protect the motherland. In 1916, novice Zachariah was drafted and sent to the army. He was seen off by Elder Gerasim who, when blessing him, said that they were seeing each other for the last time in this life. Along with his division, Zachariah was transferred to Belarus. Pressed by the Germans, the soldiers settled in the Pinsk marshes, holding this position for six months in extreme circumstances. Due to the constant dampness, Zachariah's legs became diseased. He developed chronic eczema that would plague him for the rest of his life. Later, thrombophlebitis appeared—gaping sores that would take a long time to heal, causing severe pain. It is almost impossible to cure this disease; the wound closes only for a while, but soon opens up again. Through his elder's prayers, Zachariah was placed in a detail that protected supply lines and did not participate in military action. God kept His faithful son safe.

After demobilization in 1919, Zachariah returned once again to the hermitage. Elder Gerasim had already departed to the Lord by this time and Zachariah's further growth in the spiritual life was led by Elder Nectarios, the abbot of the hermitage.

THE TAKING OF MONASTIC VOWS

In June 1920, Zachariah was tonsured into the rassaphore,[6] and in March 1921 he was tonsured a monk[7] in honor of Martyr Zenobius, Bishop of Aegea (commemorated on October 17/30). Before the giving of the vows, Abbot Nectarios wished all the future monks to lead an angelic life but warned that the hermitage might soon be closed. He declared that those who wish to be tonsured would be allowed to, yet those who were unprepared to suffer trials could still refuse. As Vladyka recalled many years later, all those gathered remained steadfast in their decision. Zachariah took his vows at a difficult time, understanding all the future trials of his chosen path.

Twenty-five miles from the hermitage in the village of Putivl on the Seyma River stood the hermitage's mills. With the blessing of Archimandrite Nectarios, Monk Zenobius drove grain to the mill and then flour back to the hermitage. In the turbulent times of the Civil War it was quite dangerous to transport carts with bread.

Usually, the caravan consisted of five or six carts. When these transports were led by Monk Zenobius, the carts would arrive unharmed. As Vladyka Zenobius later recalled, the hermitage had to surrender a bag of sugar only once, but the rest of the consignment was delivered unharmed. Monk Zenobius meekly complied with everything that the abbot blessed. Subsequently, Vladyka Zenobius repeatedly emphasized the great power of a blessing in all obediences.

Once, he was summoned to the abbot's cell. Shortly afterward, a cell attendant walked in with scissors, a comb, and razors. Monk Zenobius sat in a chair while the cell attendant shaved off his hair and beard. As Vladyka Zenobius remembered, he said nothing and did not ask anything, just meekly sat on the chair and waited to see what would happen next. After that, he was told to remain in his cell. Brother Zenobius was very upset, could not calm down or figure out why this had happened. Time passed slowly. Relying only on God's will, he came to the abbot in the evening at the appointed time. The abbot was silent, took off Brother Zenobius's robe and gave him a suit to try on. Zenobius began to put on the trousers and jacket, yet his hands would not obey. He thought the time had come for him to leave the hermitage.

Then Father Nectarios told him to harness the horses and drive the wagon to the main residence. When Monk Zenobius again entered the abbot's cell, Father Nectarios, who had just finished praying, said that having tested Zenobius, he decided to give him an important job that only he could complete. This disguise and change of appearance was intended to ensure that no one paid any attention to him. Then the abbot blessed Zenobius and asked him to drive a man who had emerged from an adjacent room. Being a skilled driver, showing ingenuity and skill, Zenobius fulfilled this request even though it was dangerous, because all of Ukraine was ruled by outlaws at that time. It turned out that he was driving a hierarch. Before parting, the bishop said "You saved a hierarch; therefore you will be a hierarch." These prophetic words came true thirty-five years later. Even so, before this would happen he had to endure many trials and hardships, privations, libel, and slander, all of which made him courageous and wise. Strength of will, faith, and prayer helped him follow his path without complaint. These events show that at the very beginning of his monastic vocation Zenobius learned to cut off his self-will and live in humility.

CLOSURE AND DEVASTATION OF THE GLINSK HERMITAGE

In 1922 the hermitage was closed. Young Communists (*komsomols*) destroyed everything, even the stone walls of the hermitage. The monks dispersed, and some of them were shot and killed. The Glinsk Hermitage was literally wiped off the face of the earth. The monastic cemetery was destroyed, and crosses from the graves were pulled out. Twenty years later, in 1942, the hermitage was reopened. "The elders gathered once again around Abbot Nectarios, who was living nearby hoping to see the future reopening of the hermitage and collecting icons, books, and vestments."[8] The hermitage was open only until 1961. When a new wave of persecution began, the Glinsk Hermitage was closed for the second time.

However, in 1922, with the blessing of the elders, Monk Zenobius took a consecrated antimins[9] and traveled to Abkhazia.

CHAPTER 3

Priesthood
and Confession of Faith

ORDINATION TO PRIESTHOOD

Having arrived in Sukhumi, Father Zenobius learned that the Dranda Assumption Monastery was still open and entered it. This monastery was the second largest in Abkhazia in terms of its number of inhabitants and significance after New Athos.[1] The Assumption Cathedral of the Dranda monastery was built in the eleventh century. After the closing of New Athos, its monks moved to Dranda. An agricultural community was established there that was joined by the monastery's monks, thus delaying its closure. Inhabitants of the monastery met Father Zenobius with joy. He was ordained a deacon there in November 1924 and on January 18, 1925, was ordained into the priesthood by Bishop Nikon of Sukhumi. All-strengthening Grace was given to him at his consecration, greatly contributing to his spiritual growth in a life of virtue. From 1925 to 1930, Father Zenobius served in the St Nicholas Church in Sukhumi.

ARREST

In 1930 Father Zenobius was arrested and held for seven months in the Rostov prison, where Father Andronicus, Father Seraphim, and other fathers from the Glinsk Hermitage were also imprisoned. Father Seraphim was later sent to Tashkent, and Father Zenobius was supposed to be exiled there also. While in prison, he contracted malaria and was hospitalized. One young doctor convened a special council of physicians to prove that because of his disease, Father Zenobius could not be sent to Central Asia, where some prisoners were about to be conveyed. He told his colleagues, "Whom do you need to work in Tashkent, the living or the dead? If Zenobius Mazhuga goes there he's a dead man."[2] Fourteen priests were sent to Tashkent, while Father Zenobius was sent to the Urals. Thus the All-Good God delivered his faithful servant from certain death. Once, during interrogation, Father Zenobius asked the investigator on what charges he was being held. The investigator silently pointed to his cassock. Vladyka Zenobius wrote in his autobiography, "In 1930 I was exiled for five years to the Urals to work in the Berezniki chemical plant and then to the White Sea–Baltic Canal, from where I received an early release in 1934."[3]

On the way to the place of confinement, the prisoners were locked in a railroad car and were not given anything to drink. The reason given was that one prisoner who was sent to fetch water didn't make it back in time before the train started again. The guards assumed that he had escaped. People began to suffer from thirst and Father Zenobius began to pray for rain, and the Lord sent heavy rainfall. Hieromonk Zenobius had a wooden spoon with him, which he pushed through the window grating to collect water and let everyone take turns drinking. When Father Zenobius arrived at the place of confinement (the clergy was usually placed among criminals), he gave away all his food and belongings. The same was done by one of his companions. Someone laughed at them and asked, "What will you have tomorrow?" When that evening they returned to the barracks from work, the belongings of Father Zenobius and the person who followed his example lay on the bed. Their mocker's belongings were all stolen and even his mattress was dragged away. Once a young man who had just entered the barracks had nowhere to sleep and spread out a newspaper to lie down on the cold concrete floor. Father Zenobius and his friend cut their blankets in half and gave them to the newcomer. In the morning he said to Father Zenobius, "Father, while I am here, you will not be harmed." It turned out that this man was a criminal "authority," and he later protected Father Zenobius and his friend in many difficult situations.

IMPRISONMENT AND RELEASE

Most prisoners treated Father Zenobius with esteem, respected his priesthood, and even called him "Father." God granted him an excellent memory. He had memorized the services and therefore could serve in prison. He baptized, confessed, and buried many. A towel served as the *epitrakhil,* on which crosses were inscribed with coal. Once he heard the confession of a man who before he was a prisoner was an executioner. At night he dreamed of the people whom he killed and could not find peace. After a couple of confessions, even this man found relief.

With God's help, Father Zenobius overcame all trials and bore the name of a Christian with honor. He showed that a true believer in Christ will never be abandoned by Him. Through difficult times He helps His faithful servants and strengthens their faith.

After his early release Father Zenobius came to Rostov-on-Don to live with the family of a man who had been with him in exile and who had settled permanently in the city. Archpriest Michael Didenko remembers that this family still lives in Rostov and continues to honor the memory of Vladyka Zenobius. Upon his return to Rostov-on-Don, Father Zenobius learned that his elder Father Andronicus was exiled to the North, to Vorkuta. There the Elder Andronicus lived in the house of the concentration camp's director, completing various tasks, even doing the laundry and cooking food.

In Rostov-on-Don[4] Father Zenobius served with the blessing of the ruling bishop Theophan in St Sofia's Church from 1934 to 1936. When persecution of the clergy began again, he returned to Abkhazia.

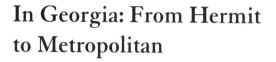

CHAPTER 4

In Georgia: From Hermit to Metropolitan

HERMIT OF THE CAUCASUS MOUNTAINS

The Caucasus Mountains, like the Egyptian desert, have long served as a place of ascetic *podvig* for Christians who have fully dedicated themselves to God. This land was consecrated by the apostle of Christ, Simon the Zealot, through his apostolic preaching and martyrdom. As the years passed becoming centuries, these mountains remained a welcome refuge for those whose souls were thirsting for solitary prayer. Sheltered in caves and wooden shacks, it seemed to them that the forest, swift rivers, and mountains were all part of an enormous monastic cell, where every creature of God could continually glorify his Creator.

Father Zenobius came to Sukhumi, yet he could not register[1] despite the fact that he owned a house there. During that difficult time, only the solitary path of the eremitic remained for those who wanted to continue the monastic way of life. He founded a small monastic community in the mountains. Among the desert fathers there he had a high reputation. Many turned to him for spiritual guidance.

During this period of his life, Father Zenobius felt the true joy of a special closeness to God. After the hermitage closed, the Glinsk elders struggled in the mountains of Abkhazia. They spiritually nourished the desert fathers who fled to Abkhazia and settled near Lake Amtkel during the persecution of Christ's Church. The elders, in addition to Father Zenobius, were Father Seraphim (Romantzov), Father Andronicus (Lukash), Archimandrite Pimen, Archimandrite Philaret, Hieromonk Nicholas, and others.

The fathers would make bread crackers and crush them into crumbs to store them easily. Before eating, the crumbs would be soaked in hot water or tea. This small monastery was home not only to the Glinsk elders, but also to elders of the Kiev-Pechersk Lavra, Pochaev, and other monasteries. Throughout his life, Vladyka Zenobius fondly remembered the days spent in the Caucasus Mountains. Even after Vladyka settled in Tbilisi, he helped the monks who continued their ascetic feats there.

After the Bolsheviks discovered and broke up this monastic community, Father Zenobius lived for some time in the Greek settlements near Sukhumi. Remembering his sewing obedience in the Glinsk Hermitage, he sewed clothes for free, which greatly endeared him to the Greeks. It should be noted that during the time he spent in the Greek villages, Father Zenobius learned to speak Greek fluently. When Vladyka lived in the Greek village of Georgievka, an incident happened that he would often later recount to his family.

One day, when hiding in the woods from the Bolsheviks, he found a comfortable place to rest and fell asleep, not suspecting that this was a bear den. Father Zenobius woke up at the sound of cracking branches and rustling leaves. It was a bear. The frightened monk surrounded himself with dry branches. His matches were damp and at first he could not light a fire, but the last match did its job. While calling on God for help, Father Zenobius lit a fire, tossing branches and twigs into it. Only then did he realize that this cozy place was a bear den. Miraculously, the bear left him alone. Later, Father Zenobius was awakened by a boy, who brought him food and said that his father would like to invite him into their home. During breakfast, Hieromonk Zenobius related the incident, but the head of the family, a hunter, laughed at him and said that he had imagined everything. The priest held his ground. In order to dissuade Father Zenobius, the hunter proposed to walk to the place. Upon arriving, the hunter saw the broken and trampled bushes, bear droppings, and, convinced of the story's truth, he said, "Yes, Father Zenobius, St Nicholas saved you, you are alive only through his intercession and protection. In all my hunting experience this is the only case where the bear left his lair without punishing the trespasser."[2] This happened on the night of May 9/22, the eve of St Nicholas and the Venerable Shio Mgvimskiy—both saints famous for their miracles. The fact that many people recount this wonderful event is, of course, proof enough of its authenticity.

Apparently, Father Zenobius labored in the Caucasus Mountains from 1936 to 1942. His autobiography only states that during those years he was ill and could not work, without mentioning his place of residence, something not surprising considering the difficult times he lived in. These secret monastic communities in the mountains were well known to the Georgian Catholicos-Patriarch Callistratus (Tsintsadze) and to Patriarch Melchizedek who succeeded him. It is well known that they appreciated the feats of the desert fathers and constantly prayed for them.

ARCHIMANDRITE AND RECTOR

Blessed Iberia[3] welcomed and protected more than one Russian elder for the world. The first of the Glinsk elders was Father Zenobius. After the second closing of the Glinsk Hermitage in 1961, Schema-Archimandrite Seraphim traveled to Sukhumi while Schema-Archimandrite Andronicus, with a number of Glinsk monks (Archimandrite Pimen, Archimandrite Philaret, Archimandrite Benjamin (Selivanov), Hegumen Ambrose, Hieromonk Nicholas, and others), went to Tbilisi. If one remembers that ancient Georgia is considered one of the earthly abodes of the Mother of God, while Russia has long been regarded as the Home of the Virgin Mary, it makes sense that our Orthodox countries are united like spiritual sisters under Her All-Pure Omorphorion, and therefore our relationship is closer than blood relations.

In 1942 Hieromonk Zenobius traveled for treatment to Georgia, where his documents were stolen and by God's will he met with Patriarch Callistratus. "His Holiness Patriarch Callistratus asked him for documents to verify his priesthood. Hieromonk Zenobius replied that he had no documents that show his spiritual rank and that Archbishop Paulinus (Kroshechkin) of Mogilev could confirm his priestly ordination. So His Holiness offered to ask him for confimation. Archbishop Paulinus with great joy assured Patriarch Callistratus of the priesthood of Hieromonk Zenobius."⁴ With the blessing of the Catholicos-Patriarch Callistratus, Zenobius served as an associate priest at the Zion Cathedral in Tbilisi from 1942 to 1944. In 1943, His Holiness and Beatitude Callistratus awarded him a pectoral cross.

When the Glinsk Hermitage was reopened in 1942, the surviving elders returned to their home hermitage. Among them were Fathers Andronicus and Seraphim. Hieromonk Zenobius did not return to the Glinsk Hermitage.

From 1944 to 1945, Father Zenobius served in the Mtskheta Olginskiy Hermitage. He was a delegate from the Georgian Church at the Local Council of the Russian Orthodox Church in 1945 and was present at the enthronement of Patriarch Alexey I, who gave awards to the entire Georgian delegation, including Father Zenobius, who was elevated to the rank of hegumen.

That same year, His Holiness Patriarch Callistratus sent Father Zenobius to the poorest parish in the village of Kirov of the Stepanavan district, and soon the spiritual level there increased considerably. Two years later Hegumen Zenobius was assigned to another parish. It was a cemetery church in Batumi in honor of the Holy Spirit, where he was rector from 1947 to 1950.

In 1949, Archpriest George Pilguev visited Vladyka. Father George related, "When I met him, Father Zenobius said that we will often see each other in the future and this was true. Hegumen Zenobius was transferred to Tbilisi, there becoming an archimandrite and rector of the St Alexander Nevsky Church, and then a hierarch. I was ordained in this church and all the while served with him."⁵

When on September 1, 1950, Archpriest John Lozovoy, rector of the St Alexander Nevsky Church in Tbilisi, departed to the Lord, to everyone's surprise, Patriarch Callistratus immediately called Father Zenobius from Batumi and on the evening of the same day elevated him to the rank of archimandrite and appointed him rector of the St Alexander Nevsky Church. When the Patriarch was asked why he chose Father Zenobius from among so many candidates, he replied, "This man . . . has great obedience, which is worth more than literacy and pride, and puts anyone in the first place."[6] The new rector of the St Alexander Nevsky Church was greeted with joy and the ringing of bells. He served in this church until the end of his earthly life.

In June 1952, at the suggestion of the Catholicos-Patriarch Melchizedek, Archimandrite Zenobius was included in the Holy Synod of the Georgian Church. On December 6 of the same year, due to "unceasing work" for the good of the Church, he was awarded a second archimandrite cross.

On May 27, 1954, Father Zenobius was sent on church affairs by Patriarch Melchizedek to the village of Kirov in the Stepanavan region of the Armenian Soviet Socialist Republic. When he completed his obedience and returned, Patriarch Melchizedek awarded him with the staff of an archimandrite. The Catholicos-Patriarch's order on September 20, 1954, states, "For selfless and sensible execution of the diocesan authorities' instructions I award him the right to carry an archimandrite's staff during church services, upon entering the church before liturgy, etc."[7] In November 1955, the rector of the St Alexander Nevsky Church, Archimandrite Zenobius, was named "Dean of the Russian parishes outside of Tbilisi in Kartaliniya, Kakheti, and Armenia."[8]

EPISCOPAL ORDINATION

On December 29, 1956, Archimandrite Zenobius was elected to the episcopate, and on December 30 his consecration took place. The Synod of the Georgian Church, headed by Patriarch Melchizedek, found the Russian priest worthy of such a high clerical rank. This was a historic event. "The merit of Vladyka Zenobius was his obedience to the higher spiritual authorities and in that he was an example of virtuous behavior to the Georgian clergy, teaching those around him to be like him. He had a rule—'the generous hand will never be empty!'"[9]

On March 6, 1957, Bishop Zenobius, rector of the St Alexander Nevsky Church, was appointed the second vicar of His Holiness with the title Bishop of Stepanavan.

VISIT TO THE RESTORED GLINSK HERMITAGE

The Glinsk Hermitage's Abbot Seraphim (Amelin) often invited Archimandrite Zenobius back as a monastic to the hermitage where they labored together in their youth. Father Zenobius often visited the Glinsk Hermitage in the 1950s. He visited it again between July 15 and August 15 of 1956 at the abbot's urging. The abbot hoped to convince Father Zenobius to take his place as the hermitage, as he himself was very elderly.

During this visit, Archimandrite Zenobius served a solemn liturgy in the hermitage church, held discussions, and gave spiritual advice to the brothers who were always very joyous to see him. Father Paulinus (Mishchenko) recalls, "At this insistent request of the Abbot Archimandrite Seraphim, Father Zenobius, not wanting to disappoint him, asked to give him some time for consideration. Yet in conversations with some of the brethren, he predicted that the hermitage would cease to exist."[10] Father Zenobius was very modest and therefore, when serving at the Glinsk Hermitage, he did not wear his second cross so as not to detract from the dignity of the abbot, who had only one cross.

Father Seraphim (Amelin) still hoped that Archimandrite Zenobius would return for good to become the hermitage's abbot. When Vladyka Zenobius visited the Glinsk Hermitage a year later, he firmly refused to lead the hermitage, even though the abbot and all the hermitage's brethren joined in chorus to prevail upon him. Nevertheless, Father Seraphim truly loved Vladyka Zenobius, so on Father Seraphim's deathbed in October 1958, he invited Vladyka to come to bid him farewell.

With the blessing of the Catholicos-Patriarch Melchizedek, Vladyka Zenobius visited the Glinsk Hermitage from October 17 to November 17, 1958. Archpriest George Pilguev, who accompanied Vladyka on the trip, recalled, "At this time we received a message about the death of the Abbot Schema-Archimandrite Seraphim. We flew from Tbilisi (Bishop Zenobius and I, a sinner) to Sumy through Kiev.... We met the brethren of the Glinsk Hermitage and the elders: Andronicus (Lukash) and Seraphim (Romantzov).... Metropolitan Zenobius, Schema-Archimandrite

Andronicus, and Schema-Archimandrite Seraphim are great elders and pillars of the Glinsk Hermitage.... All the brethren came to Vladyka Zenobius, all were blessed by the hierarch, and everyone was happy to see a spiritual child of the Glinsk Hermitage become a bishop. To be honest, some of the Glinsk Fathers were surprised that a simple, 'uneducated' monk was granted the high rank of a hierarch, yet for this monk obedience came first, leading him to spiritual heights."[11]

In conversation with some of the brethren, Vladyka Zenobius related that in tsarist times, when he was still a novice, a monk who was a fool-for-Christ lived in the Glinsk Hermitage and would predict the future. When novice Zachariah came to the holy fool with other brothers, the monk looked at him and said, "Why did you bring me this horse's head? This is a great man. I am not worthy to be visited by him." At that time the brothers and novice Zachariah did not understand anything, since the fool always spoke in parables. When Father Zenobius became a hierarch, he remembered the prediction of the fool-for-Christ.

At the end of 1960, the holy hierarch once again visited the Glinsk Hermitage. Archpriest Michael Didenko wrote, "Vladyka's heart always drew him to the holy place of his youth, especially to his friends from the hermitage, whom I first met at the Glinsk Hermitage."[12] Father Michael witnessed the reunion of the three elders, friends from childhood. He saw how their eyes shone with joy. Remembering this he added, "This joy involuntarily warmed my heart, as if I were an accomplice of their youth and present years."[13]

In 1961 the Glinsk Hermitage closed as Vladyka Zenobius predicted. All of the remaining elders settled in different countries. Father Seraphim went to Sukhumi, where he lived until his death. Yet even though he settled in Sukhumi, he often came to Tbilisi and participated in services. Father Andronicus first came to the city of Khasavyurt (Dagestan Autonomous Soviet Socialist Republic) of the Stavropol Diocese, to his former cell attendant Father Paulinus (Mishchenko),[14] and then was gladly received by Vladyka Zenobius. Metropolitan Zenobius truly loved Georgia, deeply revered the saints of the Georgian Church, and was greatly respected by her children.

BURDINO

On one occasion, some grieving parishioners of the Ascension Church in the Burdino village of the Lipetsk region came to visit Tbilisi. Their church, returned to the faithful in 1945, had stood half-ruined for many years, and services were held there infrequently. After their departure, Vladyka Zenobius blessed Father Vitaly (Sidorenko), who also lived in Tbilisi at that time, to go to Burdino in order to rebuild the church. With Vladyka's blessing, Father Vitaly and his cell attendant Mother Maria departed to the Lipetsk region. Upon hearing this, Father Vitaly's spiritual children were drawn to him from different parts of Russia. In the 1970s, Burdino was visited by Hierodeacon Alexey (Frolov, now Archbishop Alexey), Nicholas Vasin (Bishop Nikon from 1996), and Nicholas Moiseev (Bishop Theophylact from 2002).

"Thus by the elders' prayers 'the abomination of desolation' was abolished in this holy place, and monastic life was revived where three hundred years ago the Mother of God gathered under Her omorphorion the women's monastery of the Holy Protection. As predicted by Father Vitaly, sisters who desired the monastic life flew like doves to Burdino. All of them carried various obediences and many of them took monastic vows here."[15] Eventually a large monastic community was organized here. Many people from different parts of Russia began to visit Burdino on pilgrimages for spiritual nourishment. So through the blessing of Vladyka Zenobius and the labors of Father Vitaly, this monastery was restored.

Schema-Hegumenia Seraphima recalls, "Our dear Vladyka Zenobius visited this monastery. No one knew of his arrival ahead of time, yet all were eager to see this wondrous elder, and so the Lord granted this. One day in Burdino many priests suddenly gathered from neighboring regions and even from the Urals. Father Vitaly simply leaped with joy. He vested all the priests, told the nuns to wear their festal habits, and covered the church floor with carpets for the meeting of the hierarch. Thus we all went out to

meet the car in which Vladyka Zenobius had arrived without noti-
fying anyone, and Vladyka himself cried upon witnessing such a
miracle. Later Father Vitaly was asked, 'When did the telegram
come that informed of Vladyka's arrival?' He answered, 'As the
Lord said to the Apostles—wait, so did these fathers wait to see the
Hierarch-Elder Metropolitan Zenobius. And he flew to comfort his
children.'"[16]

Bishop Zenobius came to Burdino on his summer breaks from
1977 to 1979. After his first visit he said, "I thought I would find
only the forest and river here, yet I found love."[17] Vladyka and the
party of elders traveling with him were warmly welcomed and
were moved by the love among the sisters who lived here. Vladyka
and his retinue settled in small huts on the outskirts of the village.
"Around them grew an orchard and tall birch trees that protected
this area from prying eyes better than a high fence. Thickets of
hackberry trees, lushly blossoming in the spring, fenced the garden
from the riverside. It was a world of concentrated solitary prayer,
grace-filled quiet, and peace."[18]

Archbishop Alexey (Frolov) remembers, "I met Vladyka Zenobius in the Burdino village of the Voronezh[19] region in the summer
of 1979. He came there on a short vacation. What struck me when
I first met him, and what continued to amaze me every time I saw
him, was a combination of unusual meekness, humility, and at the
same time such greatness. I witnessed how people came to him for
a blessing and advice, and no one left uncomforted. The nuns who
had obediences in the church witnessed many cases of Vladyka's
clairvoyance."[20]

THE "GLINSK HERMITAGE" IN TBILISI

Under Vladyka Zenobius's omorphorion, "exiled monks of the
Glinsk Hermitage began to gather. Whilst some of them departed
to the mountain sketes of Abkhazia and others went to different
parishes, many of the elders stayed around Metropolitan Zenobius
in Tbilisi, spending days and nights in the Russian Cathedral of St
Alexander Nevsky. They were very honored not only by Russians,
but also by Georgians in an unending flow of people [who] came

to them for advice and consolation."[21] These were the famous and revered elders of the Glinsk Hermitage: Schema-Archimandrite Andronicus (Lukash), Schema-Archimandrite Seraphim (Romant-zov), Archimandrite Modest (Gamow), and the last abbot of the former hermitage, Hieromonk Philaret (Kudinov).

The St Alexander Nevsky church in Tbilisi truly became a "Russian island." "Vladyka united everyone around himself. Each year on the feast day of Hieromartyr Zenobius on October 30/November 12 such a multitude of brethren, spiritual children, and guests would gather that His Holiness the Patriarch [of Georgia] would say, 'Vladyka, you have a dependency of the Glinsk Hermitage here.' Not only brothers, but also simple laymen received shelter, solace, and spiritual nourishment from him."[22]

Just as the Glinsk Hermitage had witnessed an unceasing flow of people to the righteous elders, so did the elders in Georgia minister to people from all over the country who had come "to partake of the fountain of living Orthodox faith through the Glinsk elders of Christ."[23]

CHAPTER 5

The Last Years
of Earthly Life

On April 12, 1972, Vladyka Zenobius was consecrated a metropolitan by Metropolitan David (Devdariani). A year later, on September 12, 1973, Patriarch David (Devdariani) awarded Vladyka Zenobius the right to wear two panagias.

Under the direct supervision of Metropolitan Zenobius, the Russian Orthodox clergy of Tbilisi took an active part in the preparation and realization of the Twelfth Local Council of the Georgian Church on December 25, 1977, which culminated with the enthronement of His Holiness and Beatitude the Catholicos-Patriarch Ilia II. A delegation from the Russian Orthodox Church, headed by Patriarch Pimen, came to Tbilisi for the enthronement. On December 24, they all attended the All-Night Vigil at the Russian Church of St Alexander Nevsky, which was spiritually guided by Metropolitan Zenobius of Tetritzkaro. Vladyka Zenobius spiritually nourished the Russian Orthodox communities in Georgia for a long time. In recognition of his labors, Vladyka Zenobius accompanied His Holiness Ilia II during his first visit to Russia as Catholicos-Patriarch of Georgia in March 1978.

Shortly before his death, several priests came to Vladyka Zenobius from Russia. Vladyka spoke with them while Father Vitaly sat on the floor at his feet. Vladyka pointed to Father Vitaly and said, "Father Vitaly will replace us—Father Seraphim, Father Andronicus, and me." All those gathered bowed low to Vladyka Zenobius after these words. When he was dying, he repeated to Father Vitaly, "I leave you my children. Help them in tribulation, consoling all.

We will help, if God vouchsafes us boldness."[1] With these words Vladyka showed sincere care for his spiritual children. He did not leave them spiritually orphaned and wretched, but entrusted them to an experienced confessor and his spiritual son Father Vitaly. To Father Vitaly and Mother Seraphima he said, "Your elder is His Holiness Ilia, he is my son and is good." He then blessed them to stay in Georgia. Vladyka Zenobius loved Georgia and would say to his spiritual children, "Love Georgia as I have loved her."

The physician and surgeon G. A. Gzirishvili recalls, "I will not forget the last days of his life. He lay on his deathbed surprisingly calm, feeling ready to leave this life, as if [he] were somehow super-human, having dedicated his life to serving God and his people."[2] N. B. Lyapin writes, "Even during his last days when Vladyka suffered severe pain, he found the necessary strength to receive people eager to see him."[3]

Archpriest Alexander Chesnokov remembers, "Having served on July 19/August 1, 1984, on the Feast Day of St Seraphim of Sarov, he began to feel a weakness in his legs that made it difficult to walk and confined him to his cell. Yet on December 6/19 of that year, on the Feast Day of St Nicholas, he suddenly put on his cassock, went to church, and even prayed at the moleben after Liturgy. This was his last service in the church. After that day he did not leave his cell. The day before his death he was blessed with a vision. It occurred on March 7 during the day. He was feeling unwell, and so sat on his bed and prayed, feeling his imminent separation from the earthly life. This was revealed to him beforehand, since he had already predicted the day of his death…. The cook entered his cell and turning to her he said, 'Lidia, look how many children came to us, this room is full of little ones!' Of course, she did not see anything because it was revealed only to him who had reached such heights in the spiritual life."[4] Vladyka departed to the Lord on March 8, 1985, at 10:15 p.m. With him were Father Philaret and Father Benjamin, whom he asked to stay with him until his death, as well as his cell attendants Alexander and Michael Chesnokov.

After Vladyka's death, a suitcase was found under his bed that held his spiritual will and testament and his schema clothes. Only then did it become apparent that he was tonsured into the Great Schema with the name of Seraphim. In his will Vladyka Zenobius asked to be buried in his schema, according to his monastic rank. Vladyka was buried on March 14, and many who attended the funeral recalled that his body lay for seven days in the church, without decaying or beginning to smell during the entire week. He lay as if he were sleeping. The church and its territory were filled with people who came to bid farewell to the great elder. Many clergy came. Some of his spiritual children arrived in Tbilisi on his fortieth day.

More than twenty-five years have passed since the saint's death, yet candles always burn on his grave. Many of his spiritual children even now come and pray to the Hierarch and Elder Zenobius, knowing that even after his death he does not leave them and prays to God on their behalf.

During the many years of his pastoral work, Schema-Metropolitan Seraphim was awarded the Order of St Nina 1st,[5] 2nd, and 3rd[6] degrees, Order of St George 1st[7] and 2nd degree (Georgian Orthodox Church), Order of St Vladimir 1st and 2nd[8] degree (Russian Orthodox Church), Order of St Mark 2nd degree (Orthodox Church of Alexandria), and Order of Saints Cyril and Methodius 2nd[9] degree (Orthodox Church of the Czech Republic).[10]

Six months after the holy hierarch-elder passed away, on September 8, at the Trinity-Sergius Lavra in the Church of All Russian Saints (located under the Assumption Cathedral), a memorial service for Vladyka Zenobius was held with the blessing of the Abbot Archimandrite Alexey (Kutepov). It was led by Archimandrite Tikhon (Emelianov), chief editor of the *Journal of the Moscow Patriarchate*.

On October 30/November 12, 1985, on the feast day of Hieromartyr Zenobius, Patriarch Ilia II, in his speech before the memorial service at the St Alexander Nevsky Church, "compared Vladyka to a diamond that never loses its strength, no matter how long it exists, for its value cannot be diminished by time. One has only to swipe away a temporary coating of dust and it shines once again, revealing a unique glimpse of his former life, its radiance continually admired by many generations, who see in it the purity and infallibility of beauty and precious majesty, which he acquired after going through much cutting and faceting before being placed and secured in a glorious frame."[11]

After serving the panikhida on the first anniversary of the saint's repose, the head of the Georgian Church gave an inspiring sermon that resurrected the living image of Vladyka Zenobius in the memories of those gathered. He described him as an ascetic endowed by the Holy Spirit with many spiritual gifts of grace, especially with the gift of prayer. He "expressed the firm belief that the soul of Vladyka Zenobius is before the Throne of God and, having attained the 'crown of righteousness' (2 Tim 4:8), has boldness to pray for his spiritual children, for all those in this church, and for everyone who prayerfully honors his memory."[12]

It should be noted that His Holiness Ilia reveres the memory of his spiritual father to this day. On March 8, 2010, the twenty-fifth anniversary of the repose of St Zenobius (in schema Seraphim), Patriarch Ilia II served a memorial service. Many people gathered at the St Alexander Nevsky Church. In his sermon he said, "Today we remember him as a great elder and spiritual father. I believe that he is now helping us bear our heavy cross by praying for us."[13]

The holy relics of St Zenobius rest in the St Alexander Nevsky Church in Tbilisi, in front of the left altar in honor of St Nicholas the Wonder-worker of Myra in Lycia. Two inscriptions are carved on Vladyka's tomb: "May the Lord God remember thy episcopate in His kingdom" and "His Eminence Metropolitan Zenobius of Tetritzkaro, in schema Seraphim." Above his tomb, in a glass-covered niche, lies his cell icon—a copy of the miraculous Glinsk icon of the Nativity of the Mother of God. "The memory of Vladyka Zenobius will forever live in the hearts of many, many people. He truly labored diligently, kept the faith, and now a crown of righteousness is prepared for him, which God the Righteous Judge will give on that day (2 Tim 4: 7-8)."[14] Miracles occur at his shrine and even from everyday objects that belonged to him during his lifetime. Many people are healed and receive what they ask for in prayer before the icon of the Holy Hierarch-Elder Zenobius.

Part II

St Zenobius: Spiritual Father and Teacher

CHAPTER 6

Eldership and Pastoral Ministry

"You will receive the crown of glory that does not fade away" (1 Pet 5:4). Now, as before, the Lord does not leave His people, does not let them stray from the Truth, but supports them through His faithful pastors, who, by renouncing the devil and his sinful inclinations, have attained God's great and life-giving Grace, which they pour upon all those who come to them for help, even after the end of their earthly life. Such a shepherd of Christ's Church was St Zenobius. Even one encounter with this great elder of the twentieth century could make a great impression on people and encourage them to look differently at life and God's creation. It is appropriate to quote the words of G. A. Gzirishvili, a professor and surgeon: "In every person's life there are unforgettable days that remain in the memory for a lifetime. These are the days when you meet someone who by his mere presence has a profound effect on your mind, who opens your eyes to see the world differently. This is exactly what happened to me when I first met His Eminence Metropolitan Zenobius.... Each meeting produced a lasting impression on me. I changed and began to look differently at life, wealth, poverty, people, and even my patients. If my father taught me how to be a proficient physician and surgeon, Vladyka Zenobius was responsible for giving me an understanding of the human soul and a sick person's suffering. If I became a good doctor, then it is all thanks to Vladyka."[1] His soul was illuminated by grace that abundantly poured out on all those under his pastoral care. The Lord gave him the gift of discernment and Elder Zenobius opened the will of God to all those who asked.

For his faith and zealous pastoral ministry, the Lord granted Vladyka an unexpected joy: his cell was visited by the Blessed Virgin Herself. This happened in 1972. He was then seriously ill and bedridden. The doctors gave him two days or less to live. The hierarch-elder lay on his bed. Turning to the icon of the Mother of God, "Healer of the Sick," he devoted himself entirely to God's will. All over the world his spiritual children prayed for his recovery. The Most Holy Theotokos appeared to him in his cell and blessed him. Vladyka preserved the memory of this wonderful event in his heart. After this, Vladyka began to recover rapidly. "In the future, he outlived all the same doctors who had predicted Vladyka's death within two days. He lived for thirteen more years."[2]

A good pastor can only be someone who knows the True Shepherd, Christ, and who is known by Him: "I am the good shepherd; and I know My sheep, and am known by My own" (John 10:14). The holy hierarch Zenobius dedicated his whole life to serving God. As we know, the challenge of Christ's pastors is to bring the lost sheep back into the fold of the Church. It can be surely said that Elder Zenobius utterly devoted himself to this task. Thanks to the hierarch-elder, many people have become faithful children of Christ's Church.

The future saint began his journey of pastoral ministry upon entering the Glinsk Hermitage, famous for its elders. God Himself shows us the path to salvation through the Scriptures and the Holy Fathers: "Ask your father, and he will show you; your elders, and they will tell you" (Deut 32:7); "Where there is no counsel, the people fall; But in the multitude of counselors there is safety" (Prov 11:14); "Do nothing without counsel" (Sir 32:19). The venerable Philaret of Glinsk, in his book *Life Before and After the Monastic Vows*, writes that those who seek salvation should not rely on themselves, but rather with fear and trembling make their way only with the advice of spiritual fathers, "uncovering one's weaknesses and asking for their prayers."[3]

Our Lord and Savior Jesus Christ instituted pastoral ministry in the Church—pastors must fulfill and declare God's will that the Gospel be preached to all creation, so that the fruits of His sacrifice on

Golgotha can be revealed to all people around the world in order that those faithful to Him gradually reach perfection. "Elders" are "old and senior monks, remarkable for the austerity of their monastic life and their ability to lead others in the spiritual life."[4] Elders bear the divine gifts of the Holy Spirit. The Reverend Seraphim (Romantzov), seeing the spiritual unity of the Optina and Glinsk Hermitages noted, "The ancient Russian monastic tradition of eldership is most clearly expressed in the Glinsk and Optina monasteries."[5]

St Zenobius from his youth was entrusted to Elder Gerasim and grew spiritually under his guidance. After a long period of time he himself became a spiritual father and mentor to many. "For in that He Himself has suffered, being tempted, He is able to aid those who are tempted" (Heb 2:18). The task of an elder and spiritual mentor is to bring his flock into the kingdom of heaven. The elder is responsible before God for the souls entrusted to him. The Apostle Paul in Hebrews writes, "Obey those who rule over you, and be submissive, for they watch out for your souls, as those who must give account" (Heb 13:17).

One who leads others along the spiritual path can only be one who successfully has traveled this path himself. "An ascetic who effortlessly received gifts of grace due to purity of soul preserved from his childhood may not be able to lead others, for he does not know evil and has not passed though the struggle with passions, and therefore sees no evil in others. There have been cases where such elders, though being holy, harmed their disciples and even led them into spiritual blindness (*prelest*)."[6] In order to spiritually guide someone, one must have the gift of discernment. "Experience is the greater part of holiness," remarked Elder Leonid of Optina.[7]

"Those who steadily take the path of obedience to elders are soon successful in the spiritual life and achieve high levels of spiritual perfection, obtain the gift of discernment, easily ward off the devil's wiles, and moreover, feel great peace in their souls, not even fearing death. This inner peace and courage stem from the belief that their sins will be carried by their elder, to whom they have entrusted themselves by perfect obedience."[8] Pastoral ministry is a continuation of Christ the Savior's ministry.

It can be said that the responsibility of eldership was laid on Vladyka Zenobius from the moment people came to him to be taught and reinforced in the Orthodox faith. His all-embracing love and great strength of spirit attracted many. People would come to Vladyka from all over the country and abroad: some to know God's will in difficult circumstances, others for words of wisdom and spiritual guidance. Some came for consolation in sorrow. Next to Vladyka, each felt the breath of eternal life. Seeing him, people realized that his words were an expression of his way of life. He taught what he had experienced himself. His appearance alone inspired awe and encouraged a desire for the salvation of the soul. Vladyka never divided people into categories—good and bad, kind and cruel. For him all were equal. He did not deprive anyone of his attention.

CHAPTER 7

Simplicity and Humanity

Vladyka Zenobius was distinguished by unusual warmth, cordiality, and hospitality. Kind-hearted, open, and friendly, the elder knew how to sympathize and encourage each person who came to him. He found words of consolation for everyone. He was always accessible, simple, and considerate.

Valery Lyalin, who came to Tbilisi to see Metropolitan Zenobius, describes his first meeting with the elder:

Next to the church fence stood a monk conversing with old ladies wearing white kerchiefs. So I decided to question him. As I walked closer I saw that the monk was wizened and elderly. He was not richly dressed: a worn *skufia* on his head, an old shabby cassock, and bast shoes on his feet. He rested both hands on his staff. Oh, I thought, he must be some hermit from a poor monastery in the mountains. I listened and understood that it would be awkward to interrupt their conversation. They were talking about life. An elderly woman complained that her son-in-law drinks and then bitterly insults her. The monk-elder began to explain how to ward off his addiction to drinking. I waited until the end of the conversation and then asked the monk,

"In the name of Christ, forgive me, but where can I find Metropolitan Zenobius?"

The old man looked at me gently with his clear, kind eyes, and said softly, "I am Metropolitan Zenobius."

I was sincerely amazed!

"Your Grace, is it really you!?"

In Leningrad I saw metropolitans in black silk robes, white klobuks, diamond crosses, staffs encrusted with precious stones in their hands, saw how reverently they were welcomed as they stepped out of black lacquered cars, led to the church accompanied by glorious bell ringing, a line of priests, heads bowing low to them as the metropolitans graciously gave blessings with both hands to the people. And here is this poor elderly monk with a staff and in bast shoes. This was the Elder-Hierarch, a metropolitan.... So there I stood before such a holy hierarch, speechless and staring at his bast shoes.

The little elder laughed a quiet, silvery laugh. "What, are you wondering about my bast shoes? As we reach old age, we of the spiritual life are let down by our feet. We stand during services in prayer for a long time, so our legs weaken and hurt. And bast shoes are so good for the feet! I order them specifically from my spiritual children. My little bast shoes come from Russia and Ukraine, because no one knows of bast shoes here in the Georgian lands."[1]

This story of Valery Lyalin is similar to an incident with St Sergius of Radonezh, when a prince visited the Holy Trinity Monastery, wanting to see the abbot. St Sergius was digging the garden in a shabby cassock. The prince, seeing him, asked, "Where can I find the Abbot Sergius?" The saint answered, "I am Hegumen Sergius."

Archbishop Alexey (Frolov) remembers, "Vladyka would always graciously and sincerely welcome anyone who came. I never saw anyone who, upon parting with Vladyka, did not feel sadness. Vladyka loved all. He always worried for those who left and was upset if someone did not get in touch with him after they arrived."[2]

CHAPTER **8**

Blessing of the Holy Russian-Iverskaya Women's Monastery

In the 1970s there were very few open monasteries in Russia or Georgia. In the Didube village on the outskirts of Tbilisi, for example, a small house served as a monastery and was divided into two equal parts for men and women. Vladyka Zenobius's spiritual son Father Vitaly lived here and was helped by Mother Maria. When Father Vitaly did not have the opportunity to visit the church, he was blessed by Vladyka to serve Liturgy in his room, where there was a homemade altar and table of oblation. He would begin to serve at four o'clock in the morning and would end at seven o'clock in the morning. Before Liturgy, he would serve a long proskomedia, taking out particles for the living and the dead during most of the night. During the proskomedia, Mother Maria would read the commemoration books. "No one suspected that behind a little gate on an inconspicuous side street that ran along the mountain slope hides a real monastery."[1]

Nuns were tonsured there in secret. "The monastery's name was unusual, a double one—'Holy Russian-Iverskaya Convent in Honor of the Bogolubsk-"Searcher of the Lost" Icon of the Mother of God.' It was named by Vladyka Zenobius and Father Vitaly since they considered the founder to be the Mother of God Herself. The tonsured nuns lived in Tbilisi, Taganrog, Novosibirsk, Donetsk, Perm, Odessa, Voronezh, the Far East, the Donets Basin, Siberia. . . . They mostly resided in the outside world, each fulfilling their obedience by serving their neighbors wherever they were. Yet their spiritual home remained this corner on the outskirts of Tbilisi.

Patriarch Ilia called it a monastic inheritance, which must be preserved for the future."[2]

Schema-Abbess Seraphima said, "Departing to the Lord, the elders did not leave our little abode, but left us under the prayerful protection of His Holiness Patriarch Ilia II. Our sacred convent is alive and we are not forgotten no matter on what edge of the earth we are, for God protects our home, where we receive joy and consolation."[3]

Neither Vladyka Zenobius nor Father Vitaly hurried to give their blessing to enter the monastery and be tonsured, knowing that not everyone can bear the difficulties of monastic life. All were tonsured in Didube with the blessing of Vladyka. He was the one who gave new names to those tonsured. "When spiritual children came for guidance to Father Vitaly in Tbilisi, he always sent them to Vladyka first for advice, saying, 'Do as Vladyka blesses.' And there were no times when the elders' blessings differed."[4] Father Vitaly truly loved the wise Elder Zenobius and regarded his spiritual father with special reverence. Whenever he encountered Vladyka, he would fall to his knees and ask for a blessing.

Icon of St Zenobius (in schema Seraphim),
Metropolitan of Tetritzkaro

The Glinsk Hermitage

Visit to the Glinsk Hermitage

The Catholicos-Patriarch Kallistrat of All Georgia

Владыко Зиновий паломничаетъ въ г. Мцхета.

Pilgrimage from Tbilisi to Mtskheta

The St Alexander Nevsky Church in Tbilisi

Vladyka Zenobius in the altar of the
St Alexander Nevsky Church

Outside the St Alexander Nevsky Church in Tblisi,
early 1970s. From left to right: Archimandrite
Modest (Gamow), Elder Zenobious, Schema-
Archimandrite Seraphim (Romantsov), and
Schema-Archimandrite Andronicus (Lukash)

Pastoral care of the flock

The Elder Zenobius with the elders of the Glinsk Hermitage and clergy of the St Alexander Nevsky Church

In the altar of the St Alexander Nevsky Church in Tbilisi

Vladyka Zenobius, December 1979

Vladyka Zenobius with Father Innocent (Prosvirnin) on the Nativity of Christ, 1980

Vladyka Zenobius and Father Kirill (Pavlov)

Spiritual conversations

Vladyka Zenobius at the work table

Vladyka Zenobius at trapeza

Vladyka Zenobius at the work table in his cell

The Ascension Church in the Burdino village, the Lipetzk region

Celebrating Divine Liturgy

Vladyka Zenobius after Liturgy

Meeting the Catholicos-
Patriarch David
at the Tbilisi train
station: (left to right)
Archpriest George
Pilguev, Metropolitan
Zenobius, Metropolitan
Elijah, and Alexander
Chesnokov

Visit of the Georgian Orthodox Church delegation headed by the Catholicos-Patriarch
David to the Trinity-Sergius Lavra

Repose of
Schema-
Archimandrite
Andronicus
(Lukash)

Vladyka Zenobius
conversing with
Father Seraphim
(Romantzov)

Visit of the Georgian Orthodox Church delegation headed by the Catholicos-Patriarch
of All Georgia Ilia II to the Trinity-Sergius Lavra after his election as Patriarch, 1977

Venerating the relics of St Sergius of
Radonezh at Trinity-Sergius Lavra

His Eminence
Patriarch Pimen
and His Beatitude
Patriarch Ilia II
with hierarchs of
the Russian and
Georgian Churches
during Liturgy
at the Epiphany
Cathedral, the
vicarial church
of the Moscow
Patriarchs, on
March 5, 1978

The Catholicos-Patriarch Ilia II and Metropolitan Zenobius

After Liturgy at the Epiphany Cathedral, His Beatitude Patriarch Ilia II answers
His Eminence Patriarch Pimen's welcoming words, March 5, 1978

Metropolitan Alexey (Ridiger) and Metropolitan Zenobius on a visit to Burdino

Metropolitan Zenobius after a service at the St Alexander Nevsky Church

Pastor and spiritual father

The sisters of the Ascension Church in Burdino. In the center is nun Maria (Dyachenko).

In Burdino, early 1980s: (sitting left to right): Alexander Chesnokov, Schema-Archimandrite Vlasiy (Bolotov), Metropolitan Zenobius, and Schema-Archimandrite Vitaly (Sidorenko)

Vladyka Zenobius with clergy in Burdino

Gathering after trapeza

Metropolitan Zenobius of Tetritzkaro
in Tbilisi in the 1970s

Metropolitan Zenobius

Metropolitan Zenobius and Hieromonk
Vitaly (Sidorenko) in Burdino, early 1980s

At the St Alexander Nevsky Church, Tbilisi, on the name day of Vladyka
Zenobius, November 12, 1983

At the St Alexander Nevsky Church,
Tbilisi

Vladyka Zenobius with Father Vitaly,
early 1980s

Vladyka Zenobius and Father Vitaly in the altar of the St Alexander Nevsky Church on the feast day of St Seraphim of Sarov, August 1, 1983

Celebrating Divine Liturgy

The Elder-
Metropolitan
Zenobius in his
cell during the last
years of his life

Repose of Schema-Metropolitan Seraphim. His Holiness Patriarch Ilia II of All Georgia reads the Prayer of Absolution, March 14, 1985.

Parting with Vladyka

The last procession

CHAPTER 9

Spiritual Gifts: Miracles and Visions

St Zenobius was bestowed by God with the gift of insight: he could see the future as well as past events. He foresaw the fate of many of his spiritual children, warning them of possible trouble. Through God's inspiration, the Elder could see someone's inner state and knew how to lead each soul to salvation.

Vladyka repeatedly predicted priesthood to people who did not even think about it. Visiting the Burdino village along with his cell attendant Alexander, Vladyka told Alexander, "It would be very good if you went by the spiritual path." The cell attendant protested that he was very shy and pastoral care requires constant communication with people. St Zenobius replied, "You should enter the seminary. There they teach all of this." This prophecy was fulfilled a few years after Vladyka's death in 1985. Alexander entered the Moscow Theological Seminary, was ordained a deacon by Archbishop Alexander (Timofeev), and the following year His Holiness Ilia II the Catholicos-Patriarch ordained him a priest in the Zion Cathedral. After graduating from the Moscow Theological Academy, he stayed there as a teacher and assistant inspector. Archpriest Alexander Chesnokov is now a cleric of the Ekaterinodar and Kuban Diocese.

Father Alexander remembers, "According to his great life and prayers, the Lord gave him the gift of foresight and he could supplicate God for all people. I was near him for a long time and I can say that his blessing, words, and advice basically always came true. If someone disregarded his advice, then nothing went right and even more unpleasant consequences occurred."[1]

Archpriest George Pilguev related a very interesting event that confirmed Vladyka's foresight.

> One event that occurred in 1965 particularly shocked me and my family. I was given a summer vacation and at first my wife, my children, and I visited the holy places in Moscow, Zagorsk, etc. Upon returning home, we took a train ticket to visit my aunt in Tuapse. I went to Vladyka Zenobius for a blessing, but he did not bless us to take this trip. No matter how strongly I asked for a blessing, he was firm. The next day at the time when I was supposed to be traveling, I had a major heart attack. When the paramedics did a cardiogram, they explained that the only medicine they could recommend was lack of stress, and they said that I was still alive only because the attack happened at home. That is when we all realized exactly why Vladyka Zenobius did not bless our journey. We were grateful to him for his clairvoyance and foresight.[2]

When Vladyka was asked for guidance, he would turn to God in fervent prayer and ask Him to reveal His all-good will for the questioning person. The incident described by Father George testifies to this.

Monk Vitaly from Rostov-on-Don (whose name before monastic tonsure was Basil) related a remarkable story that indicates how clearly the wonderful Elders Zenobius and Vitaly foresaw the future, so that they even spoke as if it had already occurred and passed.

> Coming home from Pochaev, I urgently had to go to Tbilisi to deliver some fish. The fish was loaded onto my motorcycle and everyone was waiting for me when I arrived. I unloaded the fish and went right away to Vladyka. Unexpectedly, I met with Father Vitaly who said, "Oh, here comes Basil the servant of God. Beware, or else things will go badly: the devil is very angry with you." Beware of what? I went to Vladyka. He sat me down to dine with him; he always seated everyone at his table first thing. He himself ate very modestly, just a little bit of porridge, and you couldn't say that he ate like a hierarch. His hand was delicate, thin, and yellow as wax. He seemed to be glowing from the inside. He asked how my children, my wife, and mother-in-law were—he knew them all by name. Yet suddenly he said: "You know, Basil, we have a monk here who

got into a motorcycle crash: the result was a concussion and broken hand, he lay six months in the hospital. Sell your motorcycle, why do you need it?" I thought—he is a monk, but I'm a layman. I replied: "Your Grace, I'm like without hands without my motorcycle: I have to bring cucumbers, tomatoes, and chicken from the village to my children." I came home and gathered a full box of tomatoes in the village. While I was driving to Rostov by the main road, a bus crashed into me from a side road, I barely had time to turn my basket at it. I flew like a ball. There was a feeling as if something carried me in the air and threw me onto the grass, not the pavement, or else I would have been killed. I had a concussion, a broken bone, and lay six months in the hospital. Such were these Elders.[3]

One can see that Vladyka Zenobius and Father Vitaly complemented each other in their grace-filled ministry. If Basil from Rostov compared the words of these blessed elders, he would have paid more attention to what was said and avoided many troubles. The prophetic words of Vladyka, "our monk," were fulfilled after many years when Archimandrite Modest tonsured Basil as a monk with the name Vitaly.

Being a member of the Holy Synod of the Georgian Church, Father Zenobius participated in a meeting with the Patriarch of Alexandria, Christopher, in 1950. The delegation was accompanied by Bishop Pimen (later the Patriarch of Moscow and All Russia.) After the Liturgy in one of the Tbilisi churches, the delegations lined up for mutual greetings. Suddenly Father Zenobius walked up to the Patriarch of Alexandria and very emphatically asked to stand in the patriarch's place. (Vladyka later recalled that he did this unwillingly and completely understood the inappropriateness of his behavior.) Everyone was extremely surprised, but given the situation he was not asked for the reason, and the patriarch obeyed the request of the persistent archimandrite. Suddenly from the top row of the iconostasis an icon fell on Father Zenobius. The impact was very strong, tearing his klobuk apart. Father Zenobius became slightly faint, but there were absolutely no other negative consequences. All present in the church witnessed this event. Anger and frustration at the archimandrite were replaced with sincere respect and appreciation—all understood that thanks to Father Zenobius serious trouble had been avoided. None of those present doubted that a miracle has occurred. Vladyka later noted that through Divine Providence and his guardian angel, the life of the patriarch was preserved.

Many who knew Vladyka related that he had the gift of clairvoyance. Valentina, a spiritual daughter of Archimandrite Vitaly, related what happened after her marriage in 1972. She came to Vladyka for a blessing to travel with her husband and his mother to the sea for vacation. Valentina remembers, "I came up to Vladyka, took a blessing and said, 'Your Grace, bless my husband Volodya and me to go to the sea,' and he replied as if re-asking, 'What? Take sorrow along with you!?' This he repeated twice. All three of us went. The clairvoyant elder foresaw that my mother-in-law and I would suffer with my husband while vacationing at the sea. Such was the clairvoyant elder Vladyka Zenobius. Father Vitaly said, 'All those under his spiritual guidance and protection will be saved.'"[4]

Another occurrence once again reveals the great spiritual wisdom and insight of Elder Zenobius. Vladyka's cell attendant came to him for a blessing to buy a small plot in the countryside. Vladyka did not give his blessing, saying, "It will be useless if you plant crops there." Nevertheless, the plot was purchased.[5] Michael, the cell attendant's brother, recalls, "We had a plot where we were building a house. While periodically working on the construction, my brother and I were often detained and would come late to Vladyka Zenobius. One day Vladyka said that there is no point in this cottage house since it will be of little use to us and almost nothing will grow on the land. And thus it happened. The house was robbed several times and when we would visit our country house we would always take fruits and vegetables with us since there was practically no good harvests. After perestroika we sold it for a meager price."[6] Thus, the words of Vladyka were fulfilled.

During World War II Vladyka Zenobius received a vision. During the infamous siege of Leningrad , when the days of St Peter's city seemed to be numbered, he prayed hard for the embattled city. Vladyka related this vision to Valery Lyalin, who asked the elder whether there was any significance in the fact that January 14/27, the last day of the Leningrad siege, coincided with the feast day of St Nina, the Enlightener of Georgia. Vladyka, making the sign of the cross, answered that many were praying for the besieged city and added, "Metropolitan Elias Saliba of Mount Lebanon went into seclusion, fasted and prayed for forty days in a cave, and was visited by the Mother of God, Who said that while the Russian authorities continue to chain and bind the Church, there will be no victory over the enemy. For the country was not attacked only by the military power of Germany, but by demonic power. At the heart of the villainous plan to attack Russia was the secret pagan and occult satanic doctrine of the East in the Himalayas and Tibet. So finally when Stalin, a former seminary student, understood this and freed the Orthodox Church, Satan's hordes fell back to the West."[7]

"At that same time," continued Vladyka, "in the morning I had a vivid dream—St Nina fell on her knees before God's throne and asked the Lord to pity the besieged city's suffering people and to help defeat the enemy and adversary. All the while from her eyes rolled large tears, each the size of a grape. I understood by the vision that the Mother of God gave St Nina the holy obedience to be the protector of this besieged city."[8] In Russia it has long been thought that the saint on whose feast day occurs the victory over the enemy is the one who helped win the battle. The elder noted that "the inhabitants of the city on the Neva River as a sign of gratitude should have St Nina's icons in every church with an inscription commemorating the complete ending of the siege, so that our descendants remember and know about our sorrows and joys. And if a church is built there in memory of St Nina and all the martyrs of the siege, it will benefit the population and their descendants."[9]

Many years later, when Valery Lyalin returned from Georgia to St Petersburg, he went to the chapel of St Xenia of St Petersburg and then to the Smolensk cathedral. There he saw an icon of St Nina with an inscription in memory of the siege of Leningrad. Thus were fulfilled the words of Vladyka in the church of St Petersburg that Holy Blessed Xenia helped build during the night with her own hands.

The Lord revealed to the clairvoyant elder the day of his death. Holy Hierarch Zenobius, on the last night of his earthly life, said to his cell attendant, "I'm leaving you tomorrow." The cell attendant exclaimed in bitter sorrow, "Vladyka, what will become of me? I will perish without you." Gently consoling him, Vladyka replied, "I will depart, but there (pointing to the sky) I will pray for you." These words gave hope and softened the parting words of the elder.[10] In these recollections of people closest to the elder, we see not only the clairvoyance of Vladyka Zenobius, but also his love for his flock, his ardent care for each soul entrusted to him.

CHAPTER 10

Pastoral Qualities

The persecutions of the early twentieth century are comparable in their enormity and virulence perhaps only to the persecution of Christians in the first centuries. Like many martyrs for the faith, Father Zenobius was arrested without cause and for almost five years was imprisoned in camps where he suffered much harassment and mockery. He did not secure his martyrdom through blood, yet still he sorrowed and suffered much. Vladyka was repeatedly arrested and exiled. His humility and patience won the respect of prisoners, prison guards, investigators, and judges alike.

Father George Pilguev wrote that he had never seen Vladyka Zenobius, Father Andronicus, or Father Seraphim irritated or frustrated. They always found warm words for the faithful: "In joy rejoice together, in affliction understand your grief, but do not get discouraged. They all worthily carried their suffering in the world."[1] Father Vitaly remembered, "'Vladyka Zenobius taught me to swiftly roll like a round pebble to all people, showing with great love and patience how to bring someone to God, to awaken in them the desire to strive for eternal blessedness."[2] "Metropolitan Zenobius was a man of high culture. He read a great deal and was especially fond of books on church history, architecture, and iconography."[3]

Vladyka was meek and humble. He taught others how to live and how to love God through the example of his own life. Seeing his simplicity and humility, people began to seek these virtues themselves. Pastors of Christ's Church saw the depth of his spiritual life and tried to achieve it through their own actions. Archpriest Michael Didenko writes, "His simplicity, gentleness, and humility became a standard of behavior for me. The compunction that I felt during my first liturgy with him and throughout our acquaintance began to root itself in my conscience as well as in my pastoral work. In him was felt the upbringing of that hermitage in which he lived before taking holy orders, and this obedience infused his whole life to the very end."[4] In him were truly fulfilled the words of Christ the Savior: "Blessed are the meek, for they shall inherit the earth" (Matt 5:5).

Father Alexander Chesnokov recalls, "He never complained. He related with joy even the most difficult years of his life, never accusing or scolding anyone—it was evident that he took everything as if coming from God's Hand. He spoke with God through prayer. Vladyka Zenobius loved the Lord so much that everything was 'easy' for him and he was prepared for anything. He completely fulfilled the commandment of Jesus Christ: 'You shall love your neighbor as yourself' (Matt 19:19)."[5] St Zenobius loved God and every person. Everyone who simply spoke with him always left spiritually satisfied, feeling the grace that came from the elder. Father Alexander also notes that "the words of Vladyka Zenobius, filled with true humility and at the same time imbued with firm confidence, warmed the hearts of people, opened their spiritual eyes, enlightened their minds, led to repentance, spiritual peace, and spiritual rebirth."[6] In him were evident the words of Christ the Savior about following His commandments: "Whoever does and teaches them, he shall be called great in the kingdom of heaven" (Matt 5:19).

Remembering a meeting with Vladyka Zenobius, Archbishop Evlogiy (Smirnov) of Vladimir and Suzdal writes that, while still an archimandrite, he first saw with his "heart an extraordinary hierarch—then the archbishop of a Russian community in Georgia. Our conversation lasted less than a half an hour. Yet during this time Vladyka infused his soul's living faith into my own heart."[7]

Ketevan Zakharovna Nutzubidze related, "Our dear Vladyka Zenobius, after His Holiness Callistratus, Patriarch of Georgia, was the only one in the spiritual world who brought hope, encouragement, and relief in difficult days to all of our family and especially to my husband—the scholar Shalva Isaakovich Nutzubidze. Vladyka was treated with special regard by all the Patriarchs, from His Holiness Callistratus to His Holiness Ilia II. They revered him as a saint and always took into consideration everything he said. Shalva Isaakovich was grateful to Vladyka for his thoughtful care of the young people who always surrounded him and whom he always advised to finish institutions of higher education.... Being the kindest of the kind, Vladyka Zenobius was always glad to help a person, often before their request, as if doing it on his own initiative."[8]

Surrounding Vladyka was an atmosphere of spiritual love and grace that had a beneficial effect even on people's physical well-being, healing their bodily infirmities. "We were particularly attracted by his deep spirituality, humility, all-embracing humanity, simplicity, and discernment,"[9] notes Ketevan Zakharovna. The first thing Vladyka asked Shalva Isaakovich was to assist his young spiritual children in completing their studies at university. This academic support continued to be provided by Shalva Isaakovich until the end of Vladyka's life. "We were constantly in need of Vladyka Zenobius's prayers, always feeling the strength of his spiritual gifts. He was a true saint for us and we could always depend on his spiritual help as an intercessor to the Almighty."[10]

As St John Chrysostom writes, "The priest's soul must entirely shine with beauty, so that it can gladden and enlighten the souls that look up to him."[11] Vladyka Zenobius understood sorrows, trials, and illnesses as coming directly from God's hand. Through word and example he taught others to see the all-good providence of God. "Remembering the grievous circumstances of his life, with a face full of joy, he would say that he never grieved, but was glad for the trials, constantly praying and thanking his Heavenly Patroness for Her mercy, especially that the Mother of God vouchsafed him to serve the church in Georgia—Her earthly inheritance."[12] Seeing how the elder put his trust in God's providence and never complained, people tried to live by his example.

Ketevan Zakharovna also writes, "From our very first meeting it could be understood that Vladyka did not live for himself but for others, whose fate always worried him. With complete dedication he helped those around him both spiritually and materially."[13]

Vladyka Zenobius was a noble person. G. A. Gzirishvili recalls, "His face, voice, and every action was permeated with nobility. Thus he will be remembered and live in our hearts forever."[14]

CHAPTER 11

Spiritual Counselor

As an archpriest who was well acquainted with Vladyka Zeno-bius, Father Andronicus, and Father Seraphim—three elders who were in spiritual communication from their very youth and together passed through their monastery's joys and sorrows—Archpriest Michael Didenko writes of how each elder had a different approach to people and actions: "Vladyka Zenobius was distinguished by his administrative position and episcopal authority. Father Andronicus was a servant to all. Like St Seraphim of Sarov, the words 'My dear, Christ is Risen!' were always on his lips. He always treated repentant sinners with love and great condescension, gave them reasonable penance, taking the rest on himself. Thus he was in the hermitage, in prison, and in the outer world.... Elder Seraphim was stricter and more demanding with the repentant sinner. Yet people loved them all equally and showed love to each deservedly."[1]

Catholicos-Patriarch Ilia II, during a sermon in the St Alexander Nevsky Church on November 12, 1985, drew a parallel between large and small hearts. He said that if a person has a small heart he is unable to accommodate even his relatives and loved ones. Yet Metropolitan Zenobius had "a great all-embracing heart, able to hold inside many who came to him with problems and for advice. Each received relief and satisfaction after conversing with Metropolitan Zenobius, for he showed empathy to all and gave each visitor a part of his heart's warmth, so that the grace that radiated from Vladyka led many people to him. Patriarch Ilia II compared Vladyka

Zenobius to an unquenchable fire in the woods in the coldest winter, when a freezing traveler doomed to die and losing all hope to survive, lost in the dark woods, suddenly sees a fire and coming close to it is warmed enough to continue on his way with faith and hope."[2]

When Vladyka Zenobius and Father Andronicus conversed about how to apply strict canon law to people in certain circumstances, Father Andronicus "always advised Vladyka to follow the Lord's commandments: love everyone, even enemies. Regarding circumstances that occur in the clergy's pastoral service it is necessary to be guided by the situation and practices of the ancient fathers, understanding difficult situations in accordance with the Church traditions and canons."[3]

Ketevan Zakharovna Nutsubidze, remembering Vladyka, said, "Always considering the opinions of others, he never imposed his own opinions on them. Without words, he helped people understand their confusing situation and delusions, and through his modest way of life, his all-forgiving love confirmed the truth of the Christian religion. The power of his blessing and prayers we knew for ourselves, when in acute need Shalva Isaakovich would say, 'Run to the telegraph!' (i.e., where Vladyka's church was)."[4]

Vladyka's cell attendant recalls, "We always had a lot of guests. People came to us from all over the country. There is not a corner in the Soviet Union from where clergy and faithful did not come. Vladyka Zenobius was distinguished by simplicity and courtesy. Vladyka could find a common language with anyone, comforting them, and giving much needed advice."[5]

Yet Vladyka's kindness did not prevent him from being strict with people who willfully sinned. "At one time, being the spiritual father of the St Olga Monastery in the city of Mtskheta, he did not allow Abbess Angelina to partake of Holy Communion, since she allowed herself to be abusive to priests. Thus he calmed her stubborn nature and led her to repentance."[6]

Vladyka Zenobius was an example of evangelical service to others. His words had an extraordinary value for those listening, so people tried to drink in every word of the elder and live according to them, understanding that they were the words of God. He approached all situations with discernment and gave advice according to the person's particular situation. He sought to ensure that everyone who came to him received spiritual benefit and comfort.

Clavdia Burtovaya (from the Troitzkii village of the Rostov region) remembers, "In the early 1980s, my legs began to severely ache and I could not stand during the services. The rector of our church blessed me to go to a sanatorium on the sea, but before our trip, Paraskeva and I decided to stop in Tbilisi to visit Father Vitaly. He immediately directed us to Vladyka Zenobius to receive his blessing. Vladyka said to us, 'Fast during the first week, on the second receive holy unction, and then partake of Holy Communion—this will be your sanatorium.' We went to confession to Father Vitaly, who took us to Tbilisi's holy places and to the holy spring of St Shushanik. After this trip to Tbilisi my legs completely healed."[7] All these cases are truly a manifestation of God's grace through the prayers of Vladyka's loving heart. After all, a true miracle is God's answer to our love.

Many of those who were lucky enough to come into contact with Vladyka came to the faith. This happened in different ways. While still a young doctor, the surgeon G. A. Gzirishvili worked in his father's hospital and was sent to watch over the sick Vladyka Zenobius. The meeting with the elder made a lasting impression on him. Since Vladyka Zenobius was very sick, their meetings were frequent. Givi Aleksandrovich wrote, "My meeting with Vladyka gave me a great desire to be baptized, all the more so since Vladyka himself offered to be my godfather. Thus my second birth happened—my baptism in December of 1957. I was then 30 years old. He became my godfather and the closest person to me. After baptism, my personal life changed and I became a completely different person. I carried out the most complex surgeries with success and good results. I remember there was a patient with kidney cancer in critical condition, whom I treated and eventually cured. She and her whole family did not know how to thank me. They were Russian and I sent them to Vladyka's church saying, 'My success depends on God and my faith.'"[8]

As a shepherd who knows his sheep, Vladyka desired to help everyone. If someone sick turned to him for help in their illness,

Vladyka would direct them to a doctor friend. G. A. Gzirishvili confirmed this in his memoirs of Vladyka: "Patients who came to me from Vladyka I treated free of charge, in the name of God. Vladyka appreciated this."[9]

Nicholas Lyapin, a longtime cell attendant of Vladyka, remembers, "He was often visited by parishioners. Not refusing anyone and at any hour, he would always welcome those who came to him for advice. He was responsive, very kind, never indifferent to the misfortunes of others, and he always helped with advice, word, and deed . . . . The neighbors all loved and respected him. All church rules were followed strictly."[10]

As a spiritual guide and father, Vladyka Zenobius showed by his personal example the correct relationship between a pastor and his flock. "The first thing that attracted one's attention was his deep humility in the realization that he is nothing, yet from him flowed God's grace, abundantly given to him only through the faith of those seeking spiritual advice and guidance."[11] He would say to his spiritual children, "You know yourself that I am an ordinary person and do not deserve the Lord's attention, but according to God's commandment I must give advice to people in difficult situations." Vladyka also often quoted Jesus saying, "According to your faith let it be to you" (Matt 9:29), since this is a requirement for all good deeds. For his service to people, Elder Zenobius received the gift of spiritual discernment from God. As N. B. Lyapin remembers, "His counsel was always correct and instructive for us. People were forever grateful to him."[12]

CHAPTER 12

Guidance and Teaching

THE JESUS PRAYER

When Vladyka was asked how to say the Jesus Prayer, he answered that we "should not seek to reach some high level and particular concentration of thought, but with simplicity of heart pray to the Living God, Who is as close to us as our soul. He advised us to use minutes of solitude and to drive away thoughts whilst saying the Jesus Prayer. Vladyka considered this more important than reading spiritual books. He would repeat that the Jesus Prayer is instilled in a humble heart. Vladyka Zenobius told his close friends that he acquired the Jesus Prayer in his youth when he lived in the desert and now tried to keep it in the world."[1] One day Vladyka answered a monk who asked him how to reach salvation: "When you're alone in your cell, say the Jesus Prayer and drive away all thoughts—not only bad thoughts, but the good also. The silence of a monk is his freedom from thoughts. If you do so, you will see God's providence in your life."[2]

Blessing his spiritual children to say the Jesus Prayer, Elder Zenobius would also bless them to pray to the Holy Mother of God with the prayer "Most Holy Theotokos, save us" and the prayer that begins with "Theotokos, Virgin, rejoice...."[3]

ON NON-ACQUISITIVENESS: HELPING THOSE IN NEED

Vladyka taught non-acquisitiveness not only in word but also in deed. He advised his spiritual children not to get addicted to the riches of this world, but rather to strive to be frugal. He often recalled an incident during his life in the Abkhazia Mountains. Archpriest Alexander Chesnokov retells this event:

> In one of the huts there lived two monks. One day while fasting, they gathered herbs to make a soup. Not knowing how to cook, the ingredients they used made them both sick. The brother named Dmitry needed to go outside, but barred the door with a log after him to keep his brother safe in his cell while he was away. It rained that day and the ground was slippery. Dmitry walked alongside a cliff and it is surmised that, feeling sick, he slipped and fell off the cliff to his death.
>
> The next day some monks who lived nearby found the body and buried it. The other brother was unconscious in his cell for four days, but then regained consciousness. Suddenly, his deceased fellow monk began to appear to him at night. Without saying a word, he would stand in the corner of the cell and pray in sadness about something. This went on for several days. Completely exhausted, not knowing how to explain these visions and what to do, the monk related this to the other monks. Together they prayed for the deceased monk. However, the visions would not stop. According to a desert tradition, forty days after a monk's death a memorial service was held for the departed and then his clothes were distributed among the monks, each of them taking what they needed. One of the brothers took the monk's cassock. But since it was not his size and already quite worn out, the monk brought it to Hieromonk Zenobius to be altered, since in his youth he had learned to sew and would often help the brothers in the desert. Father Zenobius unstitched the cassock and found a 10 ruble gold coin from Tsarist times under the lining. He related this to the brotherhood. By mutual agreement, they decided to send Father Zenobius to Sukhumi so that he could sell the coin. Part of the proceeds he distributed to the poor and the other he divided among the brothers. After that, the departed monk came again to his fellow struggler, the brother who had shared his cell. His face expressed joyous relief; he bowed in thanks, and walked away. From that day, the deceased monk no longer appeared. According to monastic rules, monks cannot keep anything to themselves, since everything is common, and therefore the hidden coin gave him no rest."[4]

His Holiness and Beatitude Ilia II, in his sermon at the St Alexander Nevsky Church, mentioned the non-acquisitiveness of Elder Zenobius. In particular he noted, "No donated items or money would stay with him for long. Usually within the same day, he would distribute gifts he had received to those who were in need. He would then forget this immediately, since he did everything according to the Lord's commandment, 'when you do a charitable deed, do not let your left hand know what your right hand is doing' (Matt 6:3)."[5] Vladyka was extremely kind. "For every child who came to him he had a gift: a candy or a honey cake. If he had no candy, he would give them a ruble so that the child could buy what he wished and even collected rubles specifically for this."[6]

The Christmas celebrations at the St Alexander Nevsky Church were particularly memorable. Vladyka Zenobius gathered candies, chocolates, different treats, commemorative rubles, and banknotes of different value, for Christmas day. In the early morning, groups of parishioners as well as kliros and choir singers, subdeacons, and others who wished to glorify Christ, would line up at his cell door. For this day's event, everyone tried to learn the troparion and kontakion for the feast of Christmas. The singers learned and sang carols. As soon as the curtain opened on Vladyka Zenobius's cell windows, a group would walk up and ring the doorbell. Sister Nina, a strict elderly nun who survived the camps during the Church's persecution, would come out and lead them into a small room where Elder Zenobius awaited, and he would first start to sing the troparion: "Thy nativity, O Christ our God...." Those who came would begin to sing the troparion along with him. Then together they would sing the kontakion. The elder would give out prepared treats and money. Some were not able to learn the words of the troparion and kontakion, yet still they would enter Vladyka's cell with everyone, merging into a single whole and singing familiar phrases. Presents and rubles would be received by everyone equally. His cell doors were open all day long. Only the sound of bells announcing the beginning of Liturgy would stop the carolers.

On great feast days, the greeting of Vladyka Zenobius before the service happened right at his cell door, where priests of the

St Alexander Nevsky Church and guests awaited, as well as many parishioners and neighbors from nearby houses. Everyone truly loved and respected the elder.

Christmas services were majestic, with a large choir assisted by singers on the kliros. After the service, all those present in the church would go to Vladyka Zenobius's cell and sing Christmas carols. Vladyka would sing along and it seemed there were no chants that he was not familiar with. Then everyone would come up, receive his blessing, presents, and money that he would give in accordance to rank, merit, and needs. People would leave happy, contented, and grace-filled, having received material and spiritual gifts from the elder, thanking God that they found such a place in Tbilisi, where Christ was so wonderfully glorified. Naturally, the great number of people who wanted to see Vladyka Zenobius could not be accommodated in one day, so they were invited to come the next day, December 26/January 8, or even December 27/January 9. Everyone received gifts; no one left uncomforted. Vladyka always taught to give more rather than take, saying, "The generous hand will never be empty."

Everyone who came in contact at least once with Vladyka Zenobius noted that he was very kind and compassionate to every person who sought help and tried never to refuse anyone assistance. The elder, who knew the Scriptures well, remembered the words of Christ the Savior, Who said to the youth wishing to become perfect, "If you want to be perfect, go, sell what you have and give to the poor, and you will have treasure in heaven; and come, follow Me" (Matt 19:21). For Vladyka, giving alms was not only a Christian duty, but also an expression of sincere love and compassion. Once Vladyka Zenobius said, "I make my savings and investment in people, not in banks."[7] Often Vladyka gave charity to people secretly, which would later be found out quite by accident. Some monks recalled that while they were standing in church, Vladyka Zenobius would pass by them, give them a blessing, and at the same time quietly hand them money.

Ketevan Zakharovna Nutzubidze wrote, "Vladyka Zenobius was extremely generous in financially assisting those in need, since he knew the needs of both the clergy and parishioners. Without waiting for requests he satisfied everyone's needs, but he was strict with the fulfillment of the Church's canonical rules."[8] Vladyka Zenobius always said, "Do not keep any clothes or belongings of a person you had a passionate attachment to, because this object will remind you of your sin and become a stumbling block."[9] In order to fully understand Vladyka's ministry in this regard, it must be noted that he started his path of spiritual growth in the Glinsk Hermitage. There the holy hierarch was not only able to partake of the elders' spiritual life, but also acquired the spirit of the great ascetics. Their spiritual ascesis was directed to the utmost fulfillment of Christ the Savior's commandment: "Therefore you shall be perfect, just as your Father in heaven is perfect" (Matt 5:48).

ON OBEDIENCE

The elder-metropolitan's lifelong obedience began with his monastic vows, at the moment when there can no longer be a will of one's own, but in everything one must let "[His] will be done" (Matt 6:10). Vladyka tried to teach his spiritual children to obey their confessors. Growing spiritually in labor and obedience to the grace-filled elders, Vladyka Zenobius knew from personal experience the fruits of these virtues and consequently imparted them to others. Metropolitan Zenobius would assert, "Obedience is higher than love, for love without obedience is a passion, yet obedience, by purifying the human soul, leads it to spiritual love. In a proud and rebellious heart there cannot be love—only self-deception."[10]

Hegumen John (Samoilov) recalls that Vladyka Zenobius always focused on obedience to one's confessor. The holy hierarch noted, "Between the spiritual child and confessor there should be trust. The spiritual child's main quality is the complete surrender of his will to that of the confessor and obedience to him, adherence to his advice. Not in such a way that after asking you still hold fast to your own opinion. If you ask for counsel, you must do what your confessor tells you."[11]

ON SPIRITUAL READING

In his youth Vladyka Zenobius especially enjoyed reading the works of St John Chrysostom, in which he saw a special depth.

Metropolitan Zenobius would say, "Try not to read books of heterodox writers, even if you don't find anything wrong in them. These books have a different, heavy spirit— thus were we taught by our elders."[12]

ON PRAYER

Prayer was the breath that connected St Zenobius to the Source of life. Prayer was the actual and effective help that he showed people, calling the Lord's mercy upon them. St Demetrius of Rostov said regarding the power of prayer, "Prayer not only overcomes the laws of nature, not only is the invincible shield against visible and invisible enemies, but even restrains the all-powerful God's hand that is raised to destroy sinners."[13]

Vladyka Zenobius knew well that Christ's faithful shepherd must not only pray and care for the spiritual growth of his flock, but also teach them how to pray. When one of his spiritual children asked about his recommended prayers to the Mother of God, the holy hierarch answered that "Theotokos, Virgin, rejoice" encloses and holds everything in itself. "Now, think about it," and he would say the prayer slowly, pausing to contemplate. "Theotokos, Virgin, rejoice . . . Mary full of grace, the Lord is with Thee . . . Blessed art Thou among women . . . and blessed is the fruit of Thy womb . . . for Thou hast borne . . . the Savior of our souls."[14]

Vladyka loved the Blessed Virgin Mary and often turned to Her in fervent prayer. "When one hieromonk asked what one must do to remain faithful to Christ and overcome all trials if violent Church persecutions begin again, the Metropolitan answered, 'Pray to the Mother of God and as often as possible say the prayer 'Theotokos, Virgin, rejoice.' Anyone who reads this prayer is kept safe by the Most Holy Theotokos. I was in exile with one bishop. He was being forced to sign a document that asserted his participation in a conspiracy against the government; several other people were also listed in that document. He was tortured during the interrogation, but he withstood the torture and did not betray his brethren. This bishop told me that he constantly said the prayer 'Theotokos, Virgin, rejoice' and at night he would pray the Canon to the Virgin

Hodegetria, which he knew by heart. He related that he felt pain, but it was somehow muffled, and then he would lose consciousness. Since the persecutions yielded no result, he was finally left in peace."[15]

Once the holy hierarch said to a young monk, "Fear to fervently pray for those for whom you had a carnal passion; such prayer is not pleasing to God—it contains hidden lust. Entrust this person to God's providence and forget about them. If you accomplish this, then for your determination the Lord will not leave them without His mercy and take your silence for prayer."[16]

There are many recorded incidents of help through the prayerful intercession of the Holy Hierarch Zenobius. Here is a story that happened to his cell attendant. "The cell attendant gratefully remembered Vladyka's promise to pray for him when he was studying at the seminary a year later. One day he was suddenly and urgently summoned to Moscow and allowed to leave on his trip without the necessary documents. The seminarian hurried and upon arriving in Moscow, the person who called him said that he didn't have time to see him and asked him to wait. So the seminarian stayed in Moscow for the night, during which time a raging fire occurred at the seminary. Five of his friends burned to death, eleven received severe burns and injuries, many belongings and documents were burned."[17] Through the prayers of St Zenobius, his cell attendant survived.

In 1987, that same seminarian had some trouble at work. The conflict dragged on, with the seminarian trying to prove his innocence. It so happened that during a dinner, he sat next to the rector (now Metropolitan) Archimandrite Alexey (Kutepov). Father Alexey suddenly turned to the seminarian and said, "Vladyka Zenobius told me that you should not try to prove your innocence—and all will be well with you." No one understood anything except the seminarian. When he followed this advice, the conflict was resolved. Remarkably, Father Alexey had never seen Vladyka Zenobius and only visited his grave a year and a half after his death.

Another incident shows the power of the elder's prayer. One time a woman who apparently practiced witchcraft unexpectedly ran up to him and began to shout, "What kind of a man are you?

Nothing affects you, no matter what I do!"[18] Other cases confirmed the fulfillment of Vladyka's promise to pray for those whom he had left in this life. Shortly after his departure, Vladyka Zenobius came in a vision to one female worker of the St Alexander Nevsky Church. She was the mother of many children. During his life, Vladyka helped her financially, so that she could bring up her children without financial difficulty. This woman was much grieved after his death. Vladyka Zenobius appeared and consoled her by saying, "Do not be distressed. I am here with you during the services, but you cannot see me. Do not grieve, for with God's help you will raise the children. I will not leave you."[19] The woman, by the prayers of Vladyka, continued to work at the church. She was always assisted with food and clothing for the children. All six of her children are today well settled. Every day they come to the grave of Vladyka Zenobius, asking for a blessing and thanking him for his prayers.

ON MONASTICISM

Vladyka Zenobius spoke disapprovingly about monastics who often moved from place to place, calling them "flyers." The blessed elder knew the monastic life well, so he understood its hardships, always approaching those who wanted to live the angelic life with discernment, not blessing everyone to take monastic vows. Ketevan Zakharovna Nutzubidze said, "One time on the sorrowful path of my life, I almost decided to become a nun and, being quite sure that this would please Vladyka, rushed to share my thoughts with him. To my great astonishment, I heard instead, 'You don't have my blessing!' Even more surprising was the fact that instead of frustration I felt relief, because to fulfill this decision I would have to abandon the duties of a mother, the duties of a grandmother, abandon my garden and vineyard, which preserved for me the memory of Shalva Isaakovich. It was as if I regained this all over again thanks to Vladyka, to whom I am eternally grateful."[20]

THE IMPORTANCE OF TAKING A BLESSING

Vladyka Zenobius always referred to the great power of a blessing in all actions. At the Glinsk Hermitage he learned to live in obedience and to do everything with a blessing. For the edification of his spiritual children, the elder would often tell how, in the difficult times of the Civil War, he believed firmly in the power of his abbot's blessing that always ensured successful trips for the hermitage's food supply. Everyone knew that if monk Zenobius collected the supplies they would safely reach the hermitage, for he always added his own ardent prayers to the elder's blessing.

A blessing is also very important because in the consecration of any action there is the constant remembrance of God. Disobedience to an elder's blessings always leads to great complications. With Vladyka's blessing any matter would have a successful conclusion. Yet if the blessing was disregarded, the offender could expect trouble. "One of his spiritual children (then a young lieutenant) decided to take some bricks that lay next to his military unit for certain needs. Vladyka did not bless this, but the lieutenant did not listen. He drove the car up and began to load the bricks. Suddenly his military unit commander drove up. After seeing what was going on, he became extremely angry and began to yell at the lieutenant, who then had to endure many unpleasant moments and there were talks that he was going to be court-martialed. Repentant that he did not listen to Vladyka, he hurried to him and apologized, telling him everything that happened. Consoling him, Vladyka began to pray. It so happened that no one remembered about the incident, and the matter was hushed up and did not affect the service of the officer."[21]

One day, Vladyka's cell attendant decided to go home late at night. Vladyka did not bless this, saying that he would end up at the police station. Yet the cell attendant was very confident and left anyway. On the way home he was attacked by hooligans who hit him on the head with a stick. The policeman who was passing by arrested them and the cell attendant was also taken to the police station. Afterwards he had to speak in court as a witness against them. This took up a lot of his time, was very unnerving, and caused much discomfort. After this incident Vladyka's cell attendant carefully listened to the words of the clairvoyant Elder Zenobius.

ON *PODVIGS*

Vladyka approved of external ascetic feats, but warned not to rely solely on them. He encouraged and taught his spiritual children to be sensible, moderate, and prudent. He did not bless the radical feats of asceticism of particularly zealous monks who lived outside the hermitage, warning that they were inconsistent with the conditions of parish life in the world.

ON FOOD AND FASTING

Vladyka Zenobius said that if you are a guest, never try to explain fasting rules to your hosts. Eat what they have cooked and then go to confession. People should not have to fuss around you and ask, "Are you allowed to eat this or not? What about this?"[22]

CHAPTER 13

On Prayer and Church Services

Chosen from the womb to be a vessel of God's grace, Vladyka Zenobius could not imagine his life without the Church. He was an ascetic in the world. Vladyka said his prayer rule mostly at night, and the entire day belonged to the Church and people. Vladyka's cell attendant remembers, "Vladyka always prayed at night. He would get up at two or three in the morning and pray until the late morning. Sometimes, I would wake up and exclaim, 'Vladyka, have pity on yourself—lie down and rest.' Yet he would answer, 'Go to sleep, I have my own work to do.'"[1] He attended all of the daily services, and during the Liturgy he would take out many particles for the living and the dead, for those whom he knew and for those who needed his prayers. Although Vladyka was simple and unpretentious in his personal life, he celebrated the church services majestically and with splendor. It is rare to meet someone whose life was so closely connected with the church as was the life of Metropolitan Zenobius. The church is God's abode, everything in it is holy and has a deep spiritual meaning. Vladyka Zenobius with ardent insatiability lived and breathed the constant atmosphere of the church hymns, the prayerful appeals that became the elements of his soul. He looked after the church, always keeping it clean and tidy. In the churchyard he planted many trees.

In the circle of the church community he gathered monks who sang on the kliros and had other obediences. Many of the Glinsk monks after the hermitage's second closing found refuge with Vladyka Zenobius. "He seemed to replace the abbot for the Glinsk brethren. Some remained in Tbilisi near Vladyka at the St Alexander Nevsky Church, others left for the sketes in the mountains, others labored in parishes, and he helped all spiritually and financially, like a father caring for his children."[2] Wherever the Glinsk monks were, they always knew that they could find help and support in Vladyka Zenobius. Some of them remained in Georgia for the rest of their lives.

The ascetic feat of constant attention to oneself and true humility helped the elder acquire the heights of mental prayer and contemplation of God. For Vladyka the main prayer was the Jesus Prayer, in which he eventually reached perfection. It would continue inside of him unceasingly even during conversations. As an experienced ascetic of prayer, Vladyka Zenobius gave detailed instructions on the acquisition of this prayer to people of different positions and in various circumstances. The elder taught that, for a Christian to reach a truly prayerful condition in one's heart, hard work and perseverance are required. One cannot wait for the prayer to come on its own— one always has to compel oneself to it. Before the beginning of a prayer rule, the Christian must prepare for it: eliminate all outside thoughts, calm the senses, and remember to Whom one prays.

The very spiritual essence of prayer is the elevation of a person's mind and heart to God, and it can be constantly practiced since you can pray anytime, anywhere: on the road, at work or at rest, during conversations, while eating, in solitude or in a crowd, standing, sitting, or lying down. To obtain a constantly prayerful state of mind, Vladyka Zenobius advised repeating as often as possible in the mind short prayers such as "Lord have mercy," "Lord save me," or "Lord Jesus Christ, Son of God, have mercy on me a sinner." Yet one cannot rely on one's own efforts and must therefore ask the Lord to bestow the gift of prayer. All this was taught to him by his spiritual father and elder Monk Gerasim, who asked the Lord to grant true prayer to his spiritual children, one of whom was the future saint.

The prayer of the elder was very strong. One priest experienced a recurring torment. When he began to pray, a terrible head would suddenly appear and horrify him so much that he began to be afraid of staying at home alone. He was advised to visit Metropolitan

Zenobius. After listening to the priest's story, Vladyka told him to go home in peace. The elder promised to pray for him that evening, and after that nothing similar happened to the priest again.

Vladyka Zenobius performed the services with such reverence that Archimandrite Andronicus would exclaim, "What a joy it is that the Lord has granted me the opportunity to pray in our Hierarch's church!" Inextricably linked with the Glinsk Hermitage's spiritual brethren, Vladyka Zenobius would ask for their prayers and in return he "always prayed, asking God to bless all those from the Glinsk Hermitage."

Every day during services Vladyka was in church. If he was severely ill, he prayed in his cell. "There were times when in the evening he had a 104-degree temperature, yet in the morning he was already up for Liturgy and would even pray during the moleben afterwards. This continued in the last years of his life, when he reached his nineties. He spent his days in prayer and fasting."[3] Through the elder's prayers an event occurred that was reminiscent of a miracle of St John of Kronstadt, whose prayers resurrected a dead fetus in a woman's womb. This happened to the wife of the driver who worked at the St Alexander Nevsky Church in Tbilisi. In her abdominal cavity a large cyst was found, but she could not be operated on because of her pregnancy. Doctors told her that she could not bear the child since the cyst would choke it, and even if she did give birth, the child would be born sick. She appealed to Vladyka Zenobius. He prohibited an abortion and prayed for her. The woman gave birth to a healthy girl, and the cyst disappeared. The doctors could not explain the miracle.

The aunt of Vladyka's cell attendant became seriously ill in the 1970s. During a medical examination at work, the gynecologist found two lumps inside of her that he suspected were malignant. She was very worried about this and, not wanting to go through surgery, she asked her sister to bring her to Vladyka Zenobius. Hearing their story, Vladyka invited them to church, where they earnestly prayed together. After a while, the woman went on a business trip to Moscow, where she decided to have another medical examination. After examining her, the physician declared her perfectly healthy. This woman recalled, "Before turning to Vladyka for help, I myself could feel the lumps. After the prayers of Vladyka Zenobius I felt well, but I still worried and, knowing that the doctors in Moscow are skilled, I went through a medical check again in order to become sure that I was perfectly healthy. Thus I was finally convinced of how strong the Elder's prayer was."[4]

One time nun Maria became very sick. She was in critical condition and was lying near death in the hospital. After praying, she fell asleep and had a vision. St Seraphim of Sarov came with some elder who gave her a prosphoron with the Iverskaya icon of the Theotokos. St Seraphim said to her, "Go and serve this elder on Mount Athos." After this vision, she recovered and became the spiritual daughter of Elder Seraphim (Romantzov). One day he told nun Maria to visit Vladyka Zenobius in Tbilisi. When she arrived and saw Vladyka Zenobius, she dropped her suitcase from surprise. In Vladyka she saw the very same elder who came to her with St Seraphim. When she went into his cell, he said, "You will now serve the Mother of God in her country of Georgia."[5]

According to Archbishop Alexey (Frolov), something occurred that made him venerate Vladyka Zenobius even more. One day during his visit to Tbilisi he felt unwell in the morning, and by the evening he felt very sick. He went to church, but there he felt even more nauseous and to his horror he saw that he was bleeding profusely. It was most likely a ruptured ulcer. Archbishop Alexey recalls, "Of course, I was very scared and called Vladyka, who came and gently chided me that I had not earlier told him about my health. He left and I quickly fell asleep after his departure. The next morning I felt so much better that after meeting Vladyka I was able to continue my journey. I returned home completely healthy."[6] Archbishop Alexey visited Vladyka Zenobius to serve with him in the St Alexander Nevsky Church. "You should have seen how Vladyka was immersed in prayer," he recalls, "and with what feeling he read the Gospel during the vigil with his quiet, but incredibly beautiful voice."[7]

Olga Nikiforovna Chesnokov recalls, "One woman broke her leg so badly that her foot was almost about to fall off, but she did not want to go to the hospital (she was afraid that there they would cut off her leg). She asked me to bring her to Vladyka Zenobius. He began to pray for her. For a while she walked on crutches and then completely recovered."[8]

When Vladyka Zenobius was in the concentration camp he was allowed to go to the woods and pray. This was a previously unheard-of sign of trust. Departure to the forest was considered tantamount to an attempted escape, and anyone who did this without authorization would have been shot on the spot. Vladyka would go to the shore of a small lake to pray on Sundays and feast days. He recalled that on a feast day of the Theotokos he received a sure sign of his release,[9] but he would not say what kind of a sign it was. From earliest childhood, Elder Zenobius loved and revered the Mother of God, and the Most Pure Virgin never left him, always supporting him. When Vladyka took the schema, he increased his prayer rule and intensified his fasting.

CHAPTER 14

Simplicity and the Impartation of Wisdom

THE METROPOLITAN'S CHAMBERS

During all thirty-five years of his ministry in Tbilisi, Vladyka Zenobius lived in a small house next to the St Alexander Nevsky Church. Vladyka's "metropolitan's chambers" consisted of two tiny rooms. G. A. Gzirishvili remembered his first visit to Vladyka: "An elderly, noble nun met me at the door and led me into a small room, in which there was an iron bed, a small table, and two chairs .... The room's walls were adorned with icons and portraits of clergy up to the very ceiling."[1] Among the many icons that were dear to his heart was an exact copy of the miraculous icon of the Nativity of the Mother of God "Pustynno-Glinskaya."

Vladyka was faithful to his monastic vows to the end of his days. All who came here were surprised that a metropolitan had such a humble abode. Once, Patriarch Melchizedek summoned Vladyka—he wanted to give him his car and offered to help him purchase a good house. Yet Vladyka Zenobius refused, saying that he must be in church every morning and evening. Later Vladyka received a house, but he gave it to Schema-Archimandrite Andronicus and continued to live in the house with the two small rooms near the church.

The elder's ascetic way of life was evident in other things as well. Even in the altar, instead of a rich episcopal chair there was a *stasidya*.[2] When the patriarch would come, the *stasidya* would be moved from the altar's right side to the left for Vladyka and a special patriarch chair would be placed there instead.

"A room and cell where only a desk, chair, bed, and two small bookshelves could fit—this served as his office and bedroom. Patriarch David V in passing once suggested building a new residence more appropriate for Vladyka's rank and title, promising that he would be driven to church and anywhere else by car. Yet Vladyka, after a pause, refused."[3] Such was his simplicity and modesty. He received all those in need of spiritual advice in his humble "metropolitan's chambers."

SPIRITUAL CHILDREN

People loved Vladyka above all for his impeccable monastic life. The elder-metropolitan was a practitioner of the unceasing Jesus Prayer, and people saw how an inner light illuminated his face. People came to Vladyka in order to receive spiritual guidance, be comforted, ease their consciences during the sacrament of confession, talk about their sorrows, and merely to ask for advice. Not only laity and monastics, but also experienced priests and spiritual fathers would come to meet the elder-metropolitan. All were welcomed, fed, consoled, and sent back home with gifts—no one left Vladyka Zenobius empty-handed.

Among the many spiritual children of Elder Zenobius were not only laity and clergy, but also church hierarchs. One of the spiritual sons of the Elder-Metropolitan Zenobius was Patriarch Ilia II, to whom Vladyka prophesied his future patriarchal ministry in Georgia while tonsuring him a monk. Among Vladyka's spiritual children were Schema-Archimandrite Vitaly (Sidorenko), Archpriest Alexander Chesnokov, Archpriest George Pilguev, Archimandrite Innocent (Prosvirnin), and many other priests of Christ's Church.

The pastoral ministry of Elder Zenobius was multifaceted. The basic principles of his pastoral care were earnest prayer, spiritual wisdom, and patience. Having God-given wisdom, he delved into the alcoves of the human heart and was able to give timely and correct advice for any particular person's salvation. It should not be forgotten that for many years Metropolitan Zenobius was a living link between the Russian and Georgian Church, serving in Georgia under five patriarchs, all of whom loved and respected him. He was also greatly respected by the Patriarchs Alexey I and Pimen of the Russian Church. In the history of the Georgian Church, this was the only case in the twentieth and twenty-first centuries when a bishop (not to mention a metropolitan) was not Georgian by birth.

We often turn back to deep Christian antiquity in order to find luminaries who serve as examples of a truly Christian life. The Lord said, "I will build My church, and the gates of Hades shall not prevail against it" (Matt 16:18). The Church of Christ is Christ Himself and the people who carry His heavy cross on their shoulders. They carry it blamelessly until their death, fulfilling the words of the Gospel, according to which a lamp is set on a stand (Mark 4:21) so that the light of our Lord Jesus Christ's teachings may illumine our path to salvation. So said Christ the Savior after His Sermon on the Mount. The Elder-Metropolitan Zenobius labored in the Glinsk Hermitage and in the Caucasus Mountains, and being tested by God, just as gold is tried in the furnace, he was strengthened spiritually. God wanted to glorify His faithful servant. In him were fulfilled the Lord's words: "Let your light so shine before men, that they may see your good works and glorify your Father in heaven" (Matt 5:16).

St Seraphim of Sarov said, "Acquire the spirit of peace and thousands around you will be saved." Schema-Metropolitan Seraphim can truly be referred to as a grace-filled elder who received plentiful divine grace through the mysterious and invisible communion of souls. He lived and taught through his words and deeds, his entire life becoming an example of faith, humility, and obedience.

Epilogue

Assimilating the spiritual life of the Glinsk elders, St Zenobius implemented it in his life while transmitting it to his spiritual children as an indication of the true path to heaven. He was a good shepherd, always taking care of his flock. Even after becoming a hierarch he did not forget his monastic vows and to the end of his days lived in a small humble cell. He uniquely combined episcopal ministry with the grace of eldership. For his meekness and humility, the Lord granted him the gift of spiritual wisdom and insight. The Catholicos-Patriarch Ilia II, remembering his spiritual father, noted, "Vladyka was a great man of prayer, a spiritual man. I continue to feel his help to this day. His was an outstanding spiritual personality.... I am very grateful that he is with us, for we truly venerate him."[1]

On August 30/September 12, 1983, the feast day of St Alexander Nevsky, His Holiness Ilia II addressed those gathered in the church with these words: "I must say, brothers and sisters, that Vladyka Zenobius is a luminary not only of our Georgian Church, but of all Orthodoxy. St Seraphim of Sarov said, 'Acquire the Holy Spirit and thousands around you will be saved.' Vladyka Zenobius is a carrier of this divine grace, exuding not an earthly warmth, but heavenly warmth that gathers around the clergy and all believers."[2]

In conclusion, the words of Archbishop Anthony (Guliashvili) about St Zenobius should be remembered: "Vladyka always set an example of obedience, an example of purity, humility, and patience.

I know that Vladyka Zenobius suffered while still a monk at the Glinsk Hermitage, undergoing persecution and troubled times during the rule of the godless, raging government. Nevertheless, he retained a love for people and most importantly—forgiveness for all."[3]

APPENDIX

Reminiscences About
Vladyka Zenobius

HIS HOLINESS AND BEATITUDE
CATHOLICOS-PATRIARCH ILIA II[1]

Much can be said of Vladyka Zenobius. Georgia saved the Glinsk monks from persecution when they were left without a hermitage. Some, including Vladyka Zenobius, come to us here, and Patriarch Callistratus received them with love. All of his spiritual ranks he received in Georgia: archimandrite, bishop, metropolitan. He was an outstanding man—wise, correct. He knew where and what to say. Vladyka took part in my own ascent in the spiritual life. When I arrived here to take monastic vows, being a second-year student of the Moscow Theological Academy, His Holiness and Beatitude Patriarch-Catholicos of All Georgia Melchizedek III instructed me to be tonsured by Vladyka Zenobius. It was April 16, 1957. Since there were no Georgian monks, no Georgians participated in my vows. The nuns were visitors, Mother Theophania particularly stood out. They covered me with a mantle. In those days, it was somehow easier to get by in Georgia. So I waited for the new name that would be given to me and heard the name Elijah (Ilia). I was Iraklius in the world and became Elijah. Iraklius is Hercules, which means physical strength and Elijah is the power of God, spiritual power. Spiritual strength replaced physical strength. Vladyka tonsured me in the St Alexander Nevsky Church. Before my tonsure, His Holiness the Patriarch called Vladyka Zenobius and said, "A student from the theological seminary will come to you. Tonsure him a monk."

I remember thinking that I would stay the night at the St Alexander Nevsky Church after my vows. The service ended. It was very hard—I was going through some internal struggle. I felt that everything was over—the world was closed for me. We went to Vladyka's cell. He gave me a skufiya and prayer rope, saying to someone, "Call for a taxi, so he can go to his apartment." I had left my living quarters a worldly man and returned in a cassock, *riasa*, and *klobuk*.[2] A relative of mine asked me, "Why are you dressed like that?" She was a religious person, but did not know church traditions. It was Tuesday of Holy Week and on Thursday I was ordained a deacon by His Holiness and Beatitude Melchizedek. On Wednesday morning, Vladyka Zenobius presented me to the Patriarch. His Holiness said, "If I had ten such young monks, I would be most happy." Yet unfortunately, I was the only one.

After ordination my inner burden disappeared, and it seemed as if I had grown wings. I did not want to leave the Zion Cathedral. All had left and I stayed alone. I cleaned up the altar and then went to venerate St Nina's cross, but when I touched the sanctuary lamp, the oil spilled all over me. I was told that this was a sign of being touched by grace, yet I worried that I would return to the academy in an oily cassock, *riasa*, and *klobuk*. Interestingly, I came home to my relative, wiped the oil with a clean towel—and saw that there were no remaining spots. In this same cassock and *riasa* I graduated from the academy. This was a miracle. Oil always leaves stains, but there were absolutely no spots left.

Vladyka Zenobius was very merciful. He helped the students and me as well. When they would come to him, he would always give them money, prayer ropes, or something else. When Patriarch David became sick, Vladyka called me in Borjomi where I was on vacation and said that the patriarch was seriously ill. He said, "Come!" Indeed, the patriarch was in the hospital. He had gangrene and the doctors were about to amputate his leg. Several bishops, Vladyka Zenobius, and I (both metropolitans) were present. We told the doctor, "Can you imagine a patriarch without a leg? No! And if you carry out the surgery, what are the chances that he will live?" The doctors answered that the chances were one out of a hundred. And he did depart. Those were very difficult days. First, such grief, and second, some people wanted to forcibly take over the patriarchate. Vladyka Zenobius was against such a course of action. I became the patriarchal locum tenens. At the Holy Synod, Vladyka was the first to name me as a candidate for succession.

Being very kind, he sent us students parcels of fruit with dried figs. We really needed fruit, for in Russia there was very little of it. Vladyka was a great man of prayer, a spiritual man. And his help I feel to this day. This was an outstanding spiritual personality. I could speak about him very much and I have many memories. He was as pure as a child. I would ask him, "How do you feel Vladyka?" He would answer, "Battered." This meant he was cold. I have two panagias and a cross with engravings that he presented to me on the day of my enthronement. I am very glad that he is with us and we truly revere him. Mother Nina was his guardian. Yet I do not remember a time when she did not let me see Vladyka. Many wanted to visit Vladyka, but she would not let them. When I arrived she would immediately let me in.

Once there was such an occurrence. After ordination, I returned to the academy. I was twenty-four then. After some time, I received a telegram: "With the blessing of His Holiness and Beatitude, the Catholicos-Patriarch of All Georgia Melchizedek III, come to Tbilisi. With brotherly love, Bishop Zenobius." I thought—what does he mean by "brotherly love"? I am a deacon and he is a bishop. It turns out that some bishops wanted to make me a bishop, but other members of the Synod said, "Why tear him away from his studies? He studies well. When he completes his education, we can then think about his episcopacy." Instead of me, Bishop Nahum was ordained in Kutaisi. I was to be appointed to the Kutaisi diocese at twenty-four years of age. Patriarch Anthony, from the royal family, became patriarch at twenty-one. You can be elderly and not be ready for this. Thank God that everything happened according to the Lord's will.

Most importantly, the Church was not ready. After the Patriarch's departure, a very challenging period began. The Patriarch should think in advance about how to prepare the Church for the change of patriarchs so the process is less painful. According to our customs, the Patriarch writes a will in which he indicates who should be the locum tenens of the patriarchal throne. His Holiness and Beatitude Catholicos-Patriarch David for some reason said to me, "I indicated you in my will." I answered, "Why are you telling me this?" When he died, the will could not be found, so there were some who wanted to seize the patriarchal throne and even wrote a telegram to Brezhnev and Kuroyedov in Moscow that Ilia is an anti-Soviet agitator, etc. Vladyka Zenobius always supported me.

He was a very farsighted person. Though having no higher education, he was wise and peaceful. If something went wrong, he would be silent. I remember this happened during one of the sessions of the Synod, during which Metropolitan Shio declared that Vladyka Nicholas and Vladyka [Zenobius] should be deprived of their rank. He spoke loudly and Vladyka quietly said to me, "He is very cruel." Vladyka Zenobius was a merciful and compassionate person. He was in exile, yet he never talked about it. We would talk about the present and future.

We have two icons: St Nicholas and St George the Great Martyr. I call them the "members of the Synod." They are always on the table and we always pray to them. I remember that for such abusive words toward the two hierarchs, we wanted to remove this metropolitan from the Batumi cathedra. As he was speaking loudly, I prayed to the icon of St Nicholas in my soul: "You will manage everything!" Suddenly that metropolitan got up and left of his own accord.

The Ukrainian Church canonized Vladyka Zenobius on March 12/25, 2010 along with Father Seraphim and Father Andronicus. Metropolitan Zenobius spent most of his life on Georgian soil. In the future, he will also be canonized here. Thus I often think about Vladyka Zenobius—my spiritual father who unceasingly supported me. And now, I repeat, he helps me carry my heavy cross.

Tbilisi, 2010

METROPOLITAN HILARION (ALFEYEV) OF VOLOKOLAMSK

I was fifteen years old when I first came to Georgia and became acquainted with the life of this country. It must be said that the time was difficult, since they were Soviet times—the beginning of the 1980s. Then in Russia church life was in every sense very limited, but in Georgia, at least it seemed so to visitors, church life was in full swing. A lot of young people gathered around the Holy Catholicos-Patriarch Ilia II. Church services were held, as well as molebens with the reading of poetry translated into Georgian, Georgian poetry (Chavchavadze and others) was read, and many choruses sang. There was a feeling of a very rich and active spiritual life. At that same time when visiting Georgia, I first heard about Metropolitan Zenobius, who was the spiritual father of the Catholicos-Patriarch Ilia II and whom everyone revered not only as a clergyman and hierarch, but also as an elder. Thousands of people, not only from Georgia but also from Russia and all around the world, came to him for spiritual guidance. Once I happened to see Vladyka Zenobius. I came with my mother to his church and saw an elderly man of medium height with lively and very kind eyes. As I recall, he was in a light blue cassock. Vladyka invited us into his cell. It was in a fairly modest house, a humble little room, all adorned with icons. The elder talked to us about the spiritual life. Now I cannot remember what he said, since I was very young then. All the details of this conversation faded from memory, but his image, so bright and spiritually strong, remains in my heart. It seems to me that this man had a very special destiny, for he had the unique combination of the strictness of episcopal ministry and the grace of eldership. His uncommon humility, his extraordinary prayerfulness, his peculiar self-absorption and yet an openness to all who came to him was simply amazing, and I think this strongly attracted people to him. I am sure that the memorable Schema-Metropolitan Seraphim (before his departure he took the schema) prays for all of us before the throne of God.

Sergiev Posad, Trinity-Sergius Lavra, 2009

HEGUMEN JOHN (SAMOILOV)

I first became acquainted with Vladyka Zenobius when he came to Sergiev Posad to Father Innocent (Prosvirnin). It was the late 1970s, early 1980s. That's when I, a sinner, came for the first time to receive his blessing. Then I went twice to Tbilisi. One time Father Innocent took me with him. As I later realized, at that time Vladyka took the schema and when we were going back, Father Innocent gave me a paraman[3] that was for monastic vows. I keep it to this day. Then I came again by myself while on vacation just to speak with Vladyka Zenobius, to witness this elder. I immediately felt that this person was special. What surprised me in him? Firstly, of course it was his profound humility, gentleness, and meekness. People often ask me: how does meekness differ from humility? It seems to me that Vladyka was endowed with the virtue of meekness and humility—he was a model of meekness.

I will never forget the church service, which I as a layman was able to attend in the St Alexander Nevsky Church in Tbilisi when Vladyka served. He was very simple. And he seemed to be everyone's father. Any priest who served could come up to him and ask him about something. There was a certain gracious and comfortable atmosphere that always surrounded those who prayed during Liturgy with Vladyka Zenobius. Following Liturgy, Vladyka would always invite the clergy to trapeza. I was also honored with an invitation. Trapeza was always very prayerful. There was no idle talk. Vladyka would tactfully give spiritual advice to all those present. Serious issues and modern life were discussed, but most often there were spiritual conversations about the salvation of our souls.

Once I was in the St Alexander Nevsky Church during a marriage sacrament. Vladyka did not serve and entrusted this service to a parish priest. He himself at that moment prayed fervently for the young couple. At the end of the service, he said some very insightful words to them, including advice on how to live in order to keep the family together, how to live to always love each other, and how to love God. Christ must stand at the head of the created domestic church. He said a few words about the wife's obedience to her husband and the husband's wisdom. He must be sensitive, courageous, honest, and reasonable to wisely manage, like a priest, his home church.

During my stay in Tbilisi, I asked Vladyka some questions about my personal life. I can say that Vladyka's answers to my questions played a decisive role for me. Any words of such a person are received with a special feeling of gratitude.

Vladyka always focused on obedience to one's spiritual father. Between a spiritual child and a confessor there must be complete trust. The main thing that is required of a spiritual child is the complete surrender of his will to that of the confessor, obedience to him, and adherence to his advice. You should not ask him for advice in order to remain steadfast in your own opinion. If you ask, you then must do as your spiritual father says.

Vladyka was not very wordy, yet his life and relationship to those around him was much more eloquent than any sermon. We had a living model of the ideal pastor, even more, an archpastor—a person with unusual spiritual experience. St Macarius the Great was visited by several elders who asked him questions, yet one remained silent. "Why are you silent?" asked the saint, to whom the elder replied, "I need only to look at you." I did not need to ask many questions, for I already knew something about the spiritual life. The very way of life was truly important for me and it has remained in my conscience, in my mind. That is enough.

Everyone who was around Vladyka sincerely loved him: the deceased Schema-Archimandrite Vitaly, Archimandrite Innocent, and many others. For example, Father Vitaly always said, "By the prayers of our Vladyka, O Lord, have mercy on us!" assuming Vladyka Zenobius. Very often, giving us spiritual guidance during conversations, he would thus exclaim about Vladyka Zenobius. It could be felt that they were both elders: Vladyka Zenobius and Father Vitaly. All saw Vladyka as the father, even though they labored together. It is very relevant and vital that the modern pastor understands those who stand before him. After all, everything begins with obedience. It is a terrible thing when there is no respect for the bishop or abbot. Yet when there is obedience and the young respect the old, there is always peace, harmony, and love.

Father Vitaly related much about the life of Vladyka Zenobius, yet I do not remember everything. He truly respected him as a spiritual father and did everything with his blessing. He even came here (to Sergiev Posad) for treatment only with the blessing of Vladyka

Zenobius. He lived here with Father Innocent also with the blessing of Vladyka. He even departed to Christ the same way—he went to Tbilisi. A succession of eldership was always felt. Vladyka Zenobius was Father Innocent's spiritual father. Thanks to Father Innocent, I, a sinner, met Vladyka Zenobius. As far as I know, when Father Innocent had problems (two of his assistants left the *Journal of the Moscow Patriarchate*), the question arose of who was to take their place. Father Vitaly was asked and he named two of his spiritual children, whom Vladyka Zenobius blessed also. In such cases Father Innocent would always take blessings. Even when he bought a car, he also took the blessing of Vladyka Zenobius. Of course, in such cases, whenever you need pastoral advice in order to decide something, it is always important to take a blessing.

Sergiev Posad, Trinity-Sergius Lavra, 2009

NOTES

Introduction

1. Quotation from Tikhon (Emelyanov) and Michael Didenko, "His Eminence Zenobius, Metropolitan of Tetritzkaro," *Journal of the Moscow Patriarchate* 6 (1985), 59.

2. Because it was not widely known that Metropolitan Zenobius took the schema with the name of Seraphim before his repose, the elder will be referred to as Zenobius.

3. Ilia II (Ghudushauri-Shiolashvili), "Memoirs" (audio recording, 2010), *author's archives.*

4. Father Kirill (Pavlov) was born September 8, 1919, in Makovskiye Vyselki, Ryazan Oblast, Russia. One of the most respected elders of the Russian Orthodox Church, he is a living Russian Orthodox Christian mystic, elder, wonder-worker and archimandrite. He was the confessor of the Trinity-Sergius Lavra, and in particular to Patriarch Alexey II and the previous patriarchs Alexey I and Pimen.

5. Father John (Krestiankin) was archimandrite of the Pskov Caves Monastery of the Russian Orthodox Church. He was born in 1910 in the city of Oryol and departed to Christ in 2006. He is one of the most respected elders of the Russian Orthodox Church. Many cases of Father John's clairvoyance and wonder-working were recorded.

Chapter 1

1. Vladyka Zenobius, in his autobiographies and various official forms, called himself Zachariah Akimovich. In all

publications devoted to St Zenobius, his patronymic is written as Ioakimovich.

2. According to the Glinsk Hermitage's 1918 recordings, Metropolitan Zenobius was born in 1895.

3. For more details, see: G. Platonov, "This Year's Appearance of the Nativity of the Holy Virgin Icon and Its Abode in the Glinsk Hermitage of Glukhov," *Kursk Diocesan Journal* 20 (1879), 982–96.

4. Alexander Chesnokov, *The Glinsk Hermitage and Its Elders* (Sergiev Posad: Trinity-Sergius Lavra, 1994), 38.

5. Alexander Chesnokov, "The Great Elder and Hierarch Metropolitan Zenobius of Tetritzkaro." *Orthodox Voice of Kuban* 7:55 (1995), 5.

Chapter 2

1. Valery Lyalin, *The Glinsk Hermitage in Tbilisi: Heavenly Birds* (St Petersburg, 2006), 243.

2. Alexander Chesnokov, *The Glinsk Hermitage and Its Elders* (Sergiev Posad: Trinity-Sergius Lavra, 1994), 7.

3. Alexander Chesnokov, "The Glinsk Hermitage and Pastoral Ministry of Its Monks," vol. 2 (PhD diss., Moscow Theological Academy, 1990), 79.

4. Ibid, 79–80.

5. Vladyka himself related this in his sermon at the Pühtitsa Convent in 1978. Living witnesses to this were Metropolitan Alexey of Tallinn and Estonia, the abbess of the convent Barbara (Klooster), nuns, and novices. For a more detailed account, see Chesnokov, "Pastoral Ministry," 80.

6. The rassaphore is the first stage of the monastic life after ceasing to be a novice. The service for making a rassaphore includes a tonsure.

7. State Archive of the Kursk region, F. 750, Interrogation no. 1, Case no. 266, L. 6 (case on the novices of the Glinsk hermitage taking monastic orders on March 16–17, 1921). In Archbishop Manuel's unpublished manuscript *Catalogue of Russian Bishops in the Last 60 Years (1897–1957)* (Cheboksary, 1959, part 3, p. 68), he states that Metropolitan Zenobius was tonsured a monk in 1917. In the *Orthodox Encyclopedia* (Moscow: Church Research Center,

2009, vol. 20, p. 157), it is also written that he became a monk on Annunciation.

8. Lyalin, *Heavenly Birds*, 244–45.

9. The antimins is a cloth with relics sown into it that is given by a bishop to a priest as his authority to serve the Divine Liturgy. The antimins is placed on the holy table in the altar.

Chapter 3

1. New Athos was a monastery close to Sukhumi, founded in 1874 by Russian monks from Mt Athos in Greece.

2. Michael Didenko, *My Memories of the Glinsk Elders*, in Alexander Chesnokov, "The Glinsk Hermitage and Pastoral Ministry of Its Monks," vol. 2 (PhD diss., Moscow Theological Academy, 1990), 9.

3. Archive of the Georgian Patriarchate, Document no. 3657, List 17 (autobiography). Previously in all articles and works it has been incorrectly stated that Vladyka Zenobius was in exile from 1936.

4. It is most likely that Father Zenobius served in Rostov-on-Don from 1934, since in his autobiography he writes that he was given early release in 1934.

Chapter 4

1. In the Soviet Union, people were not allowed to move freely about the country without official government authorization. Moving into a new city was contingent upon receiving government approval in the form of official registration, which was not always given. This was a recurring problem for faithful Orthodox Christians during the Soviet period.

2. This incident is related in multiple sources: Chesnokov, "Great Elder," *Orthodox Voice of Kuban*, 6; Didenko, *My Memories*, 89; Theophylact (Moiseev), *From Memoirs of Vladyka Zenobius*, 142; Archimandrite Rafael (Karelin), *On the Path from Time to Eternity*, 184–86.

3. Iberia is an ancient name for Georgia.

4. Paulinus (Mishchenko), *Memories of Vladyka Zenobius*, in Alexander Chesnokov, "The Glinsk Hermitage and Pastoral

Ministry of Its Monks," vol. 2 (PhD diss., Moscow Theological Academy, 1990), 72–73.

5. George Pilguev, *Memories of the Glinsk Hermitage and Its Fathers*, in Alexander Chesnokov, "The Glinsk Hermitage and Pastoral Ministry of Its Monks," vol. 2 (PhD diss., Moscow Theological Academy, 1990), 64–65.

6. Michael Didenko, *My Memories of the Glinsk Elders,* in Alexander Chesnokov, "The Glinsk Hermitage and Pastoral Ministry of Its Monks," vol. 2 (PhD diss., Moscow Theological Academy, 1990), 6.

7. Archives of the Georgian Patriarchate, Folder no. 365, Document no. 3999, L. 12 (Paper no. 507 от 27.05.1954 г.).

8. Ibid, L. 11 (Order from 30.11.1955).

9. Didenko, *My Memories,* 7.

10. Paulinus, *Vladyka Zenobius,* 69.

11. Pilguev, *Memories of Glinsk,* 63.

12. Didenko, *My Memories*, 7.

13. Ibid, 7.

14. Father Paulinus later took the schema with the name of Gurij, reposed on August 20, 2010, and was buried in the Novospassky Monastery in Moscow.

15. *On the Life of Schema-Archimandrite Father Vitaly*: *Memories of Spiritual Children and Teachings* (Moscow: Novospassky Monastery, 2008), 99.

16. Ibid, 99–100.

17. Ibid, 100.

18. Ibid, 100.

19. During the Soviet period, Lipetsk was known as the Voronezh.

20. Alexey (Frolov), *Memories of My Stay in Tbilisi with Vladyka Zenobius*, in Alexander Chesnokov, "The Glinsk Hermitage and Pastoral Ministry of Its Monks," vol. 2 (PhD diss., Moscow Theological Academy, 1990), 135.

21. Valery Lyalin, *The Glinsk Hermitage in Tbilisi: Heavenly Birds* (St Petersburg, 2006), 244–45.

22. *Father Vitaly*, 77–78.

23. Valery Lyalin, *The Glinsk Hermitage in Tbilisi: Heavenly Birds* (St Petersburg, 2006), 251.

Chapter 5

1. *On the Life of Schema-Archimandrite Father Vitaly*: *Memories of Spiritual Children and Teachings* (Moscow: Novospassky Monastery, 2008), 87.

2. G. A. Gzirishvili, *Metropolitan Zenobius of Tetritzkaro*, 137.

3 N. B. Lyapin, *Memories of Vladyka Zenobius*, in Alexander Chesnokov, "The Glinsk Hermitage and Pastoral Ministry of Its Monks," vol. 2 (PhD diss., Moscow Theological Academy, 1990), 137–40.

4. Alexander Chesnokov, "The Glinsk Hermitage and Pastoral Ministry of Its Monks," vol. 2 (PhD diss., Moscow Theological Academy, 1990), 87–88.

5. In May 1970, the Catholicos-Patriarch Ephraim II of Georgia awarded Vladyka Zenobius with the Order of St Nina. See Folder no. 365, Document no. 3999, L. 33a.

6. The fact that Vladyka Zenobius was awarded with the Order of St Nina 3rd degree has not been made known previously, but we found the order signed by the Catholicos-Patriarch Ephraim II of All Georgia himself. See Order from the Catholicos-Patriarch of All Georgia Ephraim II, no. 133 from 14.01.1964, author's archive.

7. The fact that Vladyka Zenobius was awarded with this Order was also unmentioned previously. See Order of the Catholicos-Patriarch Ephraim II of All Georgia from 09.05.1965, author's archive.

8. The Orders of St Vladimir were awarded to Metropolitan Zenobius by Patriarch Pimen in 1975 and 1978. (Archives of the Georgian Patriarchate, Folder no. 365, Document no. 3999, L. 32, 35.)

9. The Order of Saints Cyril and Methodius was awarded to Metropolitan Zenobius by the head of the Czechoslovakian Orthodox Church Metropolitan Dorotheus during his visit to St Alexander Nevsky Church in Tbilisi on October 13, 1984. See Archives of the Georgian Patriarchate, Folder no. 887, Document no. 5648, L. 25.

10. Ecclesiastical awards are a means of recognizing and rewarding the clergy and laity for their efforts and achievements for the Church. Awards may be given for pastoral, theological,

academic, administrative, spiritual, social, educational, or missionary work, but the exact criteria and system of awards vary somewhat among the Orthodox churches.

11. Chesnokov, "Pastoral Ministry," 77.

12. Alexander Chesnokov, "The Great Elder and Hierarch Metropolitan Zenobius of Tetritzkaro," *Orthodox Voice of Kuban* 7:55 (1995), 6.

13. Ilia II (Ghudushauri-Shiolashvili), "Sermon on the 25th Anniversary of Metropolitan Zenobius's Repose" (video recording, March 8, 2010), author's archives.

14. Chesnokov, "Pastoral Ministry," 89.

Chapter 6

1. Alexander Chesnokov, "The Glinsk Hermitage and Pastoral Ministry of Its Monks," vol. 2 (PhD diss., Moscow Theological Academy, 1990), 82.

2. Alexander Chesnokov, "The Great Elder and Hierarch Metropolitan Zenobius of Tetritzkaro," *Orthodox Voice of Kuban*, 7:55 (1995), 5.

3. Philaret of the Glinsk Hermitage, *Life Before and After the Monastic Vows* (Pochaev: n.p., 1910), 2.

4. John Vulpe, "Eldership as a Kind of Pastoral Care," diploma thesis (Moscow Theological Seminary, Sergiev Posad, 1992), 26.

5. Chesnokov, "Pastoral Ministry," 18.

6. Vulpe, "Eldership," 33.

7. *The First Great Optina Elder Hieromonk Leonid (in Schema Lev)* (Shamordino, 1917), 47.

8. Vulpe, "Eldership," 38.

Chapter 7

1. Valery Lyalin, *The Glinsk Hermitage in Tbilisi: Heavenly Birds* (St Petersburg, 2006), 247–48.

2. Alexey (Frolov), *Memories of My Stay in Tbilisi with Vladyka Zenobius*, in Alexander Chesnokov, "The Glinsk Hermitage and Pastoral Ministry of Its Monks," vol. 2 (PhD diss., Moscow Theological Academy, 1990), 136.

Chapter 8

1. *On the Life of Schema-Archimandrite Father Vitaly: Memories of Spiritual Children and Teachings* (Moscow: Novospassky Monastery, 2008), 84.
2. Ibid, 84–85.
3. Ibid, 85.
4. Ibid, 86.

Chapter 9

1. Alexander Chesnokov, "The Glinsk Hermitage and Pastoral Ministry of Its Monks," vol. 2 (PhD diss., Moscow Theological Academy, 1990), 84–85.
2. George Pilguev, *Memories of the Glinsk Hermitage and Its Fathers*, in Alexander Chesnokov, "The Glinsk Hermitage and Pastoral Ministry of Its Monks," vol. 2 (PhD diss., Moscow Theological Academy, 1990), 65.
3. V. Karagodin, *Archimandrite Modest: One Who Knew How to Love* (Rostov-on-Don: Satis, 2008), 85–86.
4. Valentina Stavropol, "Memories of Vladyka Zenobius" (unpublished manuscript, 2008), author's archives.
5. Alexander Chesnokov, "The Great Elder and Hierarch Metropolitan Zenobius of Tetritzkaro," *Orthodox Voice of Kuban* 7:55 (1995), 6.
6. M. N. Chesnokov, "Memories" (unpublished manuscript, 2010), author's archives.
7. Valery Lyalin, *The Glinsk Hermitage in Tbilisi: Heavenly Birds* (St Petersburg, 2006), 252.
8. M. B. Danilushkin and M. B. Danilushkina, *Life and Biographies of the Newly Canonized Saints and Ascetics, Glorified in the Russian Orthodox Church*, vol. 1 (St Petersburg: Voskresenie, 2001), 298.
9. Ibid, 298.
10. Chesnokov, "Great Elder," *Orthodox Voice of Kuban*, 6.

Chapter 10

1. George Pilguev, *Memories of the Glinsk Hermitage and Its Fathers*, in Alexander Chesnokov, "The Glinsk Hermitage

and Pastoral Ministry of Its Monks," vol. 2 (PhD diss., Moscow Theological Academy, 1990), 67.

2. *On the Life of Schema-Archimandrite Father Vitaly: Memories of Spiritual Children and Teachings* (Moscow: Novospassky Monastery, 2008), 84.

3. M. B. Danilushkin and M. B. Danilushkina, *Life and Biographies of the Newly Canonized Saints and Ascetics, Glorified in the Russian Orthodox Church*, vol. 1 (St Petersburg: Voskresenie, 2001), 300.

4. Michael Didenko, *My Memories of the Glinsk Elders*, in Alexander Chesnokov, "The Glinsk Hermitage and Pastoral Ministry of Its Monks," vol. 2 (PhD diss., Moscow Theological Academy, 1990), 45.

5. Alexander Chesnokov, "The Glinsk Hermitage and Pastoral Ministry of Its Monks," vol. 2 (PhD diss., Moscow Theological Academy, 1990), 82.

6. Ibid, 83.

7. Evlogiy (Smirnov), "Memories" (unpublished manuscript, 2008), author's archives.

8. Chesnokov, "Pastoral Ministry," 83–84.

9. K. Z. Nutzubidze, *Memories of Vladyka Zenobius*, in Alexander Chesnokov, "The Glinsk Hermitage and Pastoral Ministry of Its Monks," vol. 2 (PhD diss., Moscow Theological Academy, 1990).

10. Chesnokov, "Pastoral Ministry," 127.

11. St John Chrysostom, *Homilies*, vol. 1, book 1 (St Petersburg, 1895), 416.

12. Danilushkin and Danilushkina, *Life and Biographies*, 300.

13. Nutzubidze, *Memories of Vladyka Zenobius*, 127–28.

14. G. A. Gzirishvili, *Metropolitan Zenobius of Tetritzkaro*, 134.

Chapter 11

1. Michael Didenko, *My Memories of the Glinsk Elders*, in Alexander Chesnokov, "The Glinsk Hermitage and Pastoral Ministry of Its Monks," vol. 2 (PhD diss., Moscow Theological Academy, 1990), 78.

2. Alexander Chesnokov, "The Glinsk Hermitage and Pastoral Ministry of Its Monks," vol. 2 (PhD diss., Moscow Theological Academy, 1990), 78.

3. Didenko, *My Memories*, 11.

4. K. Z. Nutzubidze, *Memories of Vladyka Zenobius*, in Alexander Chesnokov, "The Glinsk Hermitage and Pastoral Ministry of Its Monks," vol. 2 (PhD diss., Moscow Theological Academy, 1990), 129.

5. Chesnokov, "Pastoral Ministry," 85.

6. Alexander Chesnokov, "The Great Elder and Hierarch Metropolitan Zenobius of Tetritzkaro," *Orthodox Voice of Kuban* 7:55 (1995), 6.

7. *On the Life of Schema-Archimandrite Father Vitaly: Memories of Spiritual Children and Teachings* (Moscow: Novospassky Monastery, 2008), 163.

8. G. A. Gzirishvili, *Metropolitan Zenobius of Tetritzkaro*, 131–33.

9. Ibid, 33.

10. N. B. Lyapin, *Memories of Vladyka Zenobius*, in Alexander Chesnokov, "The Glinsk Hermitage and Pastoral Ministry of Its Monks," vol. 2 (PhD diss., Moscow Theological Academy, 1990), 139.

11. M. B. Danilushkin and M. B. Danilushkina, *Life and Biographies of the Newly Canonized Saints and Ascetics, Glorified in the Russian Orthodox Church*, vol. 1 (St Petersburg: Voskresenie, 2001), 300–301.

12. Lyapin, *Memories of Vladyka Zenobius,* 138.

Chapter 12

1. Rafael (Karelin), *On the Path from Time to Eternity* (Saratov, 2008), 192.

2. Rafael (Karelin), *Mysteries of Salvation: Conversations on the Spiritual Life from Memoirs* (Moscow: Publishing House of the Metochion of the Trinity-Sergius Lavra, 2002), 374.

3. Alexander Chesnokov, "The Great Elder and Hierarch Metropolitan Zenobius of Tetritzkaro," *Orthodox Voice of Kuban* 7:55 (1995), 6.

4. Alexander Chesnokov, "The Great Elder and Hierarch Metropolitan Zenobius of Tetritzkaro," *Journal of the Voronezh Diocese* 10:30 (1992), 49–50.

5. Alexander Chesnokov, *The Glinsk Hermitage and Its Elders* (Sergiev Posad: Trinity-Sergius Lavra, 1994), 65.

6. Chesnokov, "Great Elder," *Orthodox Voice of Kuban*, 6.

7. Rafael (Karelin), *Mysteries of Salvation: Conversations on the Spiritual Life from Memoirs* (Moscow: Trinity-Sergius Lavra, 2002), 374.

8. K. Z. Nutzubidze, *Memories of Vladyka Zenobius*, in Alexander Chesnokov, "The Glinsk Hermitage and Pastoral Ministry of Its Monks," vol. 2 (PhD diss., Moscow Theological Academy, 1990), 128–29.

9. Rafael, *Mysteries of Salvation,* 374.

10. Ibid.

11. John Samoilov, "Memoirs" (audio recording, 2009), author's archives.

12. Rafael, *Mysteries of Salvation,* 374.

13. *On the Life of Schema-Archimandrite Father Vitaly: Memories of Spiritual Children and Teachings* (Moscow: Novospassky Monastery, 2008), 143.

14. Alexander Chesnokov, *The Nativity of the Holy Virgin Glinsk Hermitage and Its Famous Elders of the 20th Century* (Zagorsk, 1991), 65.

15. Rafael (Karelin), *On the Path from Time to Eternity* (Saratov, 2008), 187–88.

16. Rafael, *Mysteries of Salvation,* 374–75.

17. Chesnokov, "Great Elder," *Orthodox Voice of Kuban,* 6.

18. M. B. Danilushkin and M. B. Danilushkina, *Life and Biographies of the Newly Canonized Saints and Ascetics, Glorified in the Russian Orthodox Church*, vol. 1 (St Petersburg: Voskresenie, 2001), 299.

19. Chesnokov, "Great Elder," *Orthodox Voice of Kuban,* 6.

20. Nutzubidze, *Memories of Vladyka Zenobius,* 128.

21. Chesnokov, "Great Elder," *Orthodox Voice of Kuban*, 6.

22. Alexander Chesnokov, "Memoirs" (audio recording, Krasnodar, 2010), author's archives.

Chapter 13

1. Alexander Chesnokov "The Great Elder and Hierarch Metropolitan Zenobius of Tetritzkaro," *Orthodox Voice of Kuban* 7:55 (1995), 6.

2. Rafael (Karelin), *On the Path from Time to Eternity*. (Saratov, 2008), 189–90.

3. Alexander Chesnokov, "The Glinsk Hermitage and Pastoral Ministry of Its Monks," vol. 2 (PhD: diss., Moscow Theological Academy, 1990), 86–87.

4. M. N. Fankeeva, "Memoirs" (audio recording, 2010), author's archives.

5. Chesnokov, "Great Elder," *Orthodox Voice of Kuban*, 6.

6. Alexey (Frolov), *Memories of My Stay in Tbilisi with Vladyka Zenobius*, in Alexander Chesnokov, "The Glinsk Hermitage and Pastoral Ministry of Its Monks," vol. 2 (PhD diss., Moscow Theological Academy, 1990), 136.

7. Ibid, 135.

8. O. N. Chesnokov, "Memoirs" (unpublished manuscript, 2008), author's archive.

9. Rafael, *On the Path*, 187.

Chapter 14

1. G. A. Gzirishvili, *Metropolitan Zenobius of Tetritzkaro*, 131–32.

2. A *stasidya* is a simple wooden church chair or monastic stall.

3. M. B. Danilushkin and M. B. Danilushkina, *Life and Biographies of the Newly Canonized Saints and Ascetics, Glorified in the Russian Orthodox Church*, vol. 1 (St Petersburg: Voskresenie, 2001), 299.

Epilogue

1. Ilia II (Ghudushauri-Shiolashvili), "Memoirs" (audio recording, 2010), author's archives.

2. Alexander Chesnokov, "The Glinsk Hermitage and Pastoral Ministry of Its Monks," vol. 2 (PhD diss., Moscow Theological Academy, 1990), 85.

3. Anthony (Guliashvili), "Memoirs of Bishop Zenobius and the Glinsk Fathers in Tbilisi" (audio recording, 2010), author's archives.

Appendix

1. The transcript of the audio recording of His Holiness and Beatitude Ilia II of All Georgia is from the author's personal archive.

2. The *riasa* is a black robe worn on top of the cassock with wide openings at the arms, and the *klobuk* is a flat-topped black hat that distinguishes monks from other non-monastic clergy.

3. A paraman is a rectangular piece with a cross and the text "I bear in my body the wounds of my Lord." It is given to a monk at his tonsure and worn at all times between the shoulder blades.

BIBLIOGRAPHY

ARCHIVAL SOURCES

Archive of the Commission for Canonizations of the Ukrainian Orthodox Church. Session of the Holy Synod of the Ukrainian Orthodox Church on March 25, 2009. Journal 9.

Archive of the Georgian Patriarchate. Document 3657.

Archive of the Georgian Patriarchate. Document 3657, List 17 (autobiography).

Archive of the Georgian Patriarchate. Folder 365, Document 3999 (Personal case of Metropolitan Zenobius).

Archive of the Georgian Patriarchate. Folder 887, Document 5648.

Russian State Historical Archive. Fund (Corpus) 796. Inventory 442. Document 2754 (Report on the state of the Kursk Diocese for 1916).

Russian State Historical Archive. Fund (Corpus) 834. Inventory 4. Document 794 (Activities of the monasteries in the Kursk diocese during the present Civil War's first year, 1916).

State Archive of the Kursk region. Fund (Corpus) 750. Inventory 1. Document 266.

State Archive of the Sumskaya region. Fund (Corpus) 454. Inventory 1. Document 3.

AUTHOR'S PERSONAL ARCHIVES

Anthony (Guliashvili). "Memoirs of Vladyka Zenobius and the Glinsk Fathers in Tbilisi" (audio recording), 2010, Tblisi.

Chesnokov, Alexander. "Memories" (audio recording), 2010, Krasnodar.

Chesnokov, M. N. "Memoirs" (unpublished manuscript), 2010, Ekaterinburg.

Chesnokov, O. N. "Memoirs" (unpublished manuscript), 2008, Krasnodar.

Diplom from the Catholicos-Patriarch of All Georgia Ephraim II, no 133 from 14.01.1964.

Diplom from the Catholicos-Patriarch of All Georgia Ephraim II, from 05.09.1965.

Evlogiy (Smirnov) of Vladimir. "Memories" (unpublished manuscript), 2008.

Fankeeva, M. N. "Memoirs" (unpublished manuscript), 2010, Naro-Fominsk.

Ilia II (Ghudushauri-Shiolashvili). "Memoirs" (audio recording), 2010, Tblisi.

Ilia II (Gudushauri-Shiolashvili). "Sermon on the 25th Anniversary of Metropolitan Zenobius's Repose" (video recording), March 8, 2010, St Alexander Nevsky Church, Tbilisi.

John (Samoilov). "Memoirs" (audio recording), 2009, Sergiev Posad.

Putzko, V. "Metropolitan Zenobius (Memoirs)" (unpublished manuscript), 2007, Kaluga.

Stavropol, Valentina. "Memoirs of Vladyka Zenobius" (unpublished manuscript), 2008.

PUBLISHED SOURCES

Abkhazian Evangelist 3 (2009), 41.

Alexey (Frolov). *Memoirs of Staying in Tbilisi with Vladyka Zenobius.* In Alexander Chesnokov, "The Glinsk Hermitage and Pastoral Ministry of Its Monks." Vol. 2. PhD diss., Moscow Theological Academy, 1990.

Chesnokov, Alexander. *The Elder-Hierarch Zenobius* (Krasnodar: Krasnodarskie Izvestia, 1998).

Chesnokov, Alexander. *The Glinsk Hermitage and Its Elders.* Sergiev Posad: Trinity-Sergius Lavra, 1994.

Chesnokov, Alexander. "The Glinsk Hermitage and Pastoral Ministry of Its Monks." Vol. 2. PhD diss., Moscow Theological Academy, 1990.

Chesnokov, Alexander. "The Great Elder and Hierarch Metropolitan Zenobius of Tetritzkaro." *Journal of the Voronezh Diocese* 10:30 (1992).

Chesnokov, Alexander. "The Great Elder and Hierarch Metropolitan Zenobius of Tetritzkaro." *Orthodox Voice of Kuban* 7:55 (1995).

Chesnokov, Alexander. *The Nativity of the Holy Virgin Glinsk Hermitage and Its Famous Elders of the 20th Century.* Zagorsk: n.p., 1991.

Chesnokov, Alexander and Z. A. Chesnokov. "The Great Glinsk Elder: Metropolitan Zenobius (Mazuga) of Tetritzkaro (In Schema Seraphim)." In International Academic-Themed Conference for the 1020 Year of the Baptism of Russia. Sumy: Hellas, 2009, 36–45.

Chrysostom, John. *Homilies.* Vol. 1, bks. 1 and 2. St Petersburg, 1895.

Danilushkin, M. B., and M. B. Danilushkina. *Life and Biographies of the Newly Canonized Saints and Ascetics, Glorified in the Russian Orthodox Church.* Vol. 1. St Petersburg: Voskresenie, 2001.

Didenko, Michael. *My Memoirs of the Glinsk Fathers.* In Alexander Chesnokov, "The Glinsk Hermitage and Pastoral Ministry of Its Monks." Vol. 2. PhD diss., Moscow Theological Academy, 1990, 3–11.

The First Great Optina Elder Hieromonk Leonid (in Schema Lev). 2nd ed. Shamordino: n.p., 1917.

Georgian Orthodox Church. *Orthodox Church Calendar for 1980.* Moscow, 1979.

"The Georgian Orthodox Church: The Catholicos-Patriarch of All Georgia." In *Orthodox Encyclopedia.* Vol. 13. Moscow: Church Research Center, 2006.

Gzirishvili, G. A. *Metropolitan Zenobius of Tetritzkaro.*

John (Maslov). *Lectures on Pastoral Theology.* Moscow: n.p., 2001.

John (Maslov). *The Glinsk Hermitage: A History of the Hermitage and Its Missionary Work in the 16th–20th Centuries.* Moscow: n.p., 2007.

John (Maslov). *The Glinsk Paterikon.* Moscow: Sashmit, 1997.

Karagodin, V. *Archimandrite Modest: One Who Knew How to Love.* Rostov-on-Don: Satis, 2008.

Lyalin, Valery. *The Glinsk Hermitage in Tbilisi: Heavenly Birds*. St Petersburg: n.p., 2006.

Lyapin, N. B. *Memories of Vladyka Zenobius*. In Alexander Chesnokov, "The Glinsk Hermitage and Pastoral Ministry of Its Monks." Vol. 2. PhD diss., Moscow Theological Academy, 1990, 137–40.

Manuel (Lemeshevskiy) (Archbishop). *Catalogue of Russian Bishops in theLast 60 Years (1897–1957)*. Part 3. Unpublished manuscript, Cheboksary, 1959.

Maslov, N. V. "The Glinsk Hermitage of the Nativity of the Blessed Virgin." In *Orthodox Encyclopedia*. Vol. 11. Moscow: Church Research Center, 2006.

Maslov, N. V. *Letters Glinsk Elders*. Moscow: n.p. 2006.

Memories of the Pochaev Elder Archimandrite Achilles. Kiev: n.p., 2006, 599.

"Metropolitan Zenobius (Mazhuga)." In *Orthodox Encyclopedia*. Vol. 20. Moscow: Church Research Center, 2006.

Nikitin, V. "Election and Enthronement of His Holiness and Beatitude the Catholicos-Patriarch of All Georgia Ilia II." *Journal of the Moscow Patriarchate* 3 (1978), 9–12.

Nikitin, V. "Fraternal Visit of the Patriarch of All Georgia." *Journal of the Moscow Patriarchate* 6 (1978), 912.

Nutzubidze, K. Z. *Memories of Vladyka Zenobius*. In Alexander Chesnokov, "The Glinsk Hermitage and Pastoral Ministry of Its Monks." Vol. 2. PhD diss., Moscow Theological Academy, 1990, 127–30.

On the Life of Schema-Archimandrite Father Vitaly: Memories of Spiritual Children and Teachings. Moscow: Novospassky Monastery, 2008.

Orthodox Church Calendar for 2010. Moscow: Publishing House of the Moscow Patriarchate, 2009.

"Participation of Monasteries in the Kursk Diocese in Public Education and Charity." *Kursk Diocesan Journal* 14 (1891), 229–30.

The Parting. Metropolitan Zenobius [article in Georgian]. In Jvari Vazis, "The Lozovoy Cross," *Journal of the Georgian Patriarchate* 1 (1985).

Paulinus (Mishchenko). *Memories of Vladyka Zenobius.* In Alexander Chesnokov, "The Glinsk Hermitage and Pastoral Ministry of Its Monks." Vol. 2. PhD diss., Moscow Theological Academy, 1990, 69–73.

Philaret of the Glinsk Hermitage. *Life Before and After the Monastic Vows: Guidance for Monks.* Pochaev: n.p., 1910.

Pilguev, George. *Memories of the Glinsk Hermitage and Its Fathers.* In Alexander Chesnokov, "The Glinsk Hermitage and Pastoral Ministry of Its Monks." Vol. 2. PhD diss., Moscow Theological Academy, 1990, 62–68.

Platonov, G. "This Year's Appearance of the Nativity of the Holy Virgin Icon and Its Abode in the Glinsk Hermitage of Glukhov." *Kursk Diocesan Journal* 20 (1879).

Raphael (Karelin). *Memories.* In Alexander Chesnokov, "The Glinsk Hermitage and Pastoral Ministry of Its Monks." Vol. 2. PhD diss., Moscow Theological Academy, 1990, 12–23.

Rafael (Karelin). *Mysteries of Salvation: Conversations on the Spiritual Life from Memoirs.* Moscow: Publishing House of the Metochion of the Trinity-Sergius Lavra, 2002.

Rafael (Karelin). *On the Path from Time to Eternity.* Saratov: n.p., 2008.

Theophylact (Moses). *From Memories of Vladyka Zenobius, Metropolitan of Tetritzkaro.* In Alexander Chesnokov, "The Glinsk Hermitage and Pastoral Ministry of Its Monks." Vol. 2. PhD diss., Moscow Theological Academy, 1990, 141–44.

Tikhon (Emelyanov) and Michael Didenko. "His Eminence Metropolitan Zenobius of Tetritzkaro." *Journal of the Moscow Patriarchate* 6 (1985), 58–59.

Vazis, Jvari. "The Lozovoy Cross." *Journal of the Georgian Patriarchate* 1 (1985).

Vulpe, John. "Eldership as a Kind of Pastoral Care." Diploma thesis, Moscow Theological Seminary, Sergiev Posad, 1992, 62.

INDEX

The citations in parentheses following the page numbers refer to note numbers; for example, 81(n4) refers to the text associated with note 4 on page 81. References to pictures begin with "P"; for example, P2 refers to a picture on the second unnumbered page of the illustration section.